Scripture in Context Series

Science & the Bible

Scripture in Context Series

Science & the Bible

Modern Insights for an Ancient Text

David Instone-Brewer

LEXHAM PRESS

Science and the Bible: Modern Insights for an Ancient Text
Scripture in Context Series

Lexham Press, 1313 Commercial St., Bellingham, WA 98225
LexhamPress.com

Earlier versions of some chapters in this book appeared as articles in *Premier Christianity* magazine (www.premierchristianity.com). Used by permission.

Print ISBN 9781683594031
Digital ISBN 9781683594048
Library of Congress Control Number 2020940443

Lexham Editorial Team: Elliot Ritzema, Claire Brubaker, Kelsey Matthews
Cover Design: Owen Craft
Typesetting: Abigail Stocker

Contents

Section 4:
Humanity

Section 5:
Miracles

▼

Introduction

There are many books about the Bible and science, but this one is different. In this book I assume that both the Bible and science are sources of knowledge. I won't be seeking either to "correct" the Bible by using science or to "correct" science by using the Bible. My aim is to use science to provide additional insights that will help us choose between different ways of understanding various Bible texts. So if two different interpretations are equally founded on the text, but only one of them agrees with what we know about the natural world, then we should take this as an additional factor in its favor.

My expertise is in the Bible—especially its languages and historical background. However, I have also done a lot of academic training in the sciences. I have taken university exams (and sometimes retaken them!) in biochemistry, anatomy, physiology, psychology, sociology, pharmacology, neurology, psychiatry, microbiology, and various other -ologys. I know how to read and evaluate scientific papers, and I do my best to keep abreast of various fields. I do this because I'm immensely curious about all aspects of the natural and human world.

My experience in these two fields leads me to approach science and the Bible with a few assumptions.

HOW TO THINK ABOUT MIRACLES

My working assumption about miracles is that they are possible, though, as the Bible suggests, they are rare. Science can't be used to explain away miracles in the Bible because they are, by definition, outside the scope of scientific investigation. Since we cannot study the mechanism of an action we cannot reproduce, we can't study the mechanisms behind a once-only miracle. It is like taking a car to a mechanic to find the source of a mysterious noise that happened only once: if the mechanic can't replicate it, there is no way for him to investigate it. However, we can still use what we know from the various sciences to try to understand what actually happened as described in the Bible text, just as that mechanic might recognize what happened when you describe the circumstances.

I also assume that God's preferred method is to carry out his will by using the creation that he made. Of course, since the time of Adam and Eve, God's will is often being frustrated, so he may have to use extraordinary methods to fix things. His creation includes agents such as angels whom we can't perceive, who may be used by God to get his will done. Nevertheless, in general we should assume that God wants to get things done by using his creation—that's why he made it. This means that when investigating what God did in the Bible, we should first consider whether it could happen within the confines of what his creation is capable of—and the sciences can tell us a great deal about that.

HOW TO EVALUATE SCIENTIFIC THEORIES

When looking at science, we have to be aware that some areas are more established and certain than others. However, this doesn't mean that we should dismiss everything that is called a theory. This technical term is used for everything from the well-established theory of gravity to things as uncertain as a theory of mind. A theory is an explanation that incorporates all the currently known facts as simply as possible. It is called a theory because if other facts come along that can't be fitted into that explanation, it may need to be revised. Therefore, Newton's theory of gravity was revised when Einstein discovered that light bends around massive objects—though the refinement was so small that it doesn't make any practical difference to our everyday lives.

When science stories get into the news, it is because exciting new things have been discovered. This can give us the false impression that the world of science is always changing and that most conclusions are uncertain. The vast majority of scientific findings never need revising, so they never get into the news, though they become part of our everyday lives through technology. If all this science wasn't reliable, we'd never be able to make an electric car that is safe, or interpret signals from GPS satellites to find out where we are driving.

There is no conspiracy by scientists to pretend things are certain when they are not. Every scientist longs to find evidence that will overturn a currently accepted theory and thereby move knowledge forward—and make themselves famous. I can't imagine anyone wanting to work in science merely to find supporting evidence for what is already accepted. So the idea that scientists are motivated by a plot to undermine religion or the Bible is (as far as I can see) an unbelievable conspiracy theory. There are some antireligious scientists, and there are just as many scientists who are devout believers, but their faith or lack of it makes no difference to the scientific method. As in all professions, a few individuals cut corners to progress their careers, but they are almost certain to be found out eventually because every scientist longs to win fame by proving something wrong.

Promotion and funding come by finding new facts that change the consensus, and hopefully finding a more elegant and useful theory to describe reality.

HOW TO EVALUATE BIBLE THEORIES

This same methodology can be used to study the Bible. Just as a scientist regards facts as more important than the current theory, we should regard the text as more important than the current interpretation. If an interpretation of a particular passage agrees with some but not all other texts in the Bible, then the interpretation clearly needs to be developed further—just as scientific theories are constantly refined when new facts are discovered.

Let's attempt, for example, to elucidate a theory about answered prayer. We may start out by interpreting the Bible as saying:

God grants the prayers of his followers.

But then we read about Cornelius, whose prayers God responded to even before he became a Christian (Acts 10:4), and how God loves seekers (Heb 11:6). So we revise our interpretation to:

God grants the prayers of those who seek him.

Then we remember that God doesn't always answer prayers in the way we expect. For example, Paul asked God to release him from his "thorn in the flesh," but after praying for this repeatedly, he was told the thorn would not be removed because God was using it for his good purpose (2 Cor 12:7–9). This makes us revise our interpretation again:

God grants the prayers of those who seek him, in accordance with his good will.

Some believers, such as prosperity preachers, think that the simple interpretation we started with is correct. But most Christians incorporate the extra facts found in the Bible and revise their interpretation to encompass the whole of what the Bible says.

BIBLE + SCIENCE = BETTER UNDERSTANDING

In this book we will go a little further. We will look at the facts that we find in the Bible and add to these the findings of science. Scientific ideas help us understand how things work, and in this book I attempt to apply science to help us understand what the Bible says.

I do not want to elevate scientific knowledge above what is clearly taught in the Bible. The Westminster Confession of Faith usefully makes a distinction between those "clearly propounded" doctrines that are "necessary to be known, believed and observed for salvation" and those areas of Scripture that are "not alike plain in themselves nor alike clear unto all."[1] This book is wholly concerned with that latter group, where there is insufficient information in Scripture for us to be certain what the correct interpretation is. As I have said above, when the facts in the Bible are capable of more than one interpretation, our scientific knowledge can help us decide which interpretation is likely to be correct.

This is similar to the way that we use archaeology to help fill in the details that the Bible doesn't mention. For example, the Bible describes the Philistines dominating the Israelites because they had the technological advantage of "chariots of

---

1. Westminster Confession of Faith 1:7 (TinyURL.com/WestminsterConf). Note that this book shortens internet links using TinyURL.com to make them easier to type into the address bar of your browser.

iron" (Josh 17:16–18; Judg 1:19; 4:3, 13 ESV). But a chariot made completely of iron wouldn't be fast or agile and would often sink in the mud, so the text is difficult to understand. However, archaeology supplies the detail that although they used iron for wheel rims, hubs, and other hard-wearing parts, the rest of the chariot was built from wood to be as light as possible for speed. This additional information from archaeology doesn't correct the Bible, but it does help us understand it. And information from science can do the same.

Many books attempt to show that the Bible is true by arguing that it agrees with what scientists have found out, and others try to tell scientists they are wrong by citing interpretations of the Bible. This book tries to do something else: it seeks to use science as one of our tools to help understand what the Bible says. I'm not interested in proving anyone wrong or right; I'm interested in employing every available piece of knowledge to help understand the Bible in context. And in this book, we are going to use science to help us do that.

Section 1

▾

The Universe

1

▾

God Works by Miracles, Not Magic

In the Bible, God's miracles aren't like magic tricks—he doesn't suddenly produce things out of thin air or make something disappear in a puff of smoke, though presumably he could. The way he does work tells us a lot about what he is like.

Imagine you're participating in a supermarket dash. With family, friends, and representatives from the supermarket's headquarters looking on, the store manager gives you your instructions: "You have two and a half minutes to fill your cart with anything in the shop. Ready ... steady ... go!" Immediately you make for the checkouts and grab all the cash from the tills, then sprint to the manager's office and snatch his wallet and car keys from his jacket pocket. You're looking around for the key to the safe when he catches up with you to explain: "I meant anything that's *for sale* in the shop!"

Human language often implies things that we don't actually state. We all know that "Say no to drugs" only refers to illegal drugs rather than drugs that are medically prescribed for us. Someone might boast that they "can draw anything you can describe," but if we challenged them to draw an "inside-out circle" they'd be stumped. What they meant was, "I can draw anything that *can* be drawn."

So when the Bible says that nothing is impossible for God (Gen 18:14; Job 42:2; Jer 32:17; Matt 19:26 [= Mark 10:27 = Luke 18:27]; Luke 1:37; Mark 14:36), does it mean that God can do *anything*? Or does it mean that he can do *anything that can be done*? For instance, does it mean that God can make a mountain ride a horse? He can only do this if the mountain is no longer a mountain or the horse is no longer a horse. And does it mean that God can make me become Moses, who died before I was born? He can only do this if he overhauls the whole physics of space-time and overrides the concepts of individuals and personhood.

Would God change the way the whole universe works simply for one miracle? We can assert that he *could*, but the events recorded in the Bible suggest that he *wouldn't*. He moved water to let his people walk to the other side of the sea—but he didn't make them disappear and instantly rematerialize on the far shore. God raised some people from the dead—but he didn't turn back time so that they hadn't died. God revealed to prophets his plans for the future using visions, dreams, and words—but he didn't download the information into their brains like fully formed "memories." It's helpful to think of the Bible as describing God working within the structures of the existing universe as a craftsman, a strategist, or a gardener.

CRAFTSMAN

In the Bible we read about God using the built-in facilities of his world like a craftsman uses the tools he has made; he doesn't simply bypass the normal processes of nature as if he were a science-fiction alien or a fantasy wizard. So if we take the Bible seriously, we have to accept that this is how God chooses to act. Even in the creation narrative, God did not produce a working and populated planet with a snap of his fingers; he is described as taking time to carry out this process. Of course, the actual length of time is subject to interpretation, but the point of the text is to show that it wasn't instantaneous.

Augustine couldn't understand why God would choose to take time to create things and decided that this *wasn't* the way God worked. He assumed that, because God is omnipotent, all his actions occur instantaneously. So Augustine interpreted the six days of creation as six different descriptions of God performing a single instantaneous creation.[1] In other words, he allowed his presuppositions to overrule the clear message of the Bible text.

STRATEGIST

The creation narrative also describes God doing things in a systematic and logical order. He first makes light, then land, then plants, then seasons, then animals, then humans. One leads to the other, like a town planner who develops a new project by first laying out streets and sewers, then erecting buildings, and finally connecting water and electricity before inviting anyone to live there. We read that after creating matter, God built or "made" his creation instead of popping things into existence.[2]

Miracles in the Bible imply a similar principle. When food was provided miraculously, it came from other food—albeit very

---

1. Augustine writes in his *Unfinished Literal Meaning of Genesis*: "How can ... God need a length of time in order to complete something? ... But in [Genesis] the account of the things that God made is broken down most conveniently as if in periods of time so that the very arrangement which weaker souls could not look upon with a firm gaze could be discerned" (1:7.28; see TinyURL.com/AugustineGen1-7). He writes elsewhere in *The Literal Meaning of Genesis*: "Creation, therefore, did not take place slowly. ... There was no passage of time" (4.33.52; see TinyURL.com/AugustineGenIV).

2. The verb *asah*, "to make," is used in Gen 1:7, 11, 12, 16, 25, 26, and 31. See more in chap. 9, "Everyone Believes in Evolution."

quickly (1 Kgs 17:10–16; Matt 14:15–21).[3] When plagues descended
on Egypt, they occurred in a logical order: a plague of flies followed after all the frogs had died and left piles of corpses (Exod
8:13–16).[4] It seems that miracles use natural processes when
possible, albeit in a supernatural way. Healing miracles appear
to be instantaneous, but perhaps they happen too quickly for
humans to see the process. Occasionally they occurred more
slowly, such as when Elijah stretched himself on a dead boy three
times before the child came to life (1 Kgs 17:17–24), and when a
blind man whose sight was restored by Jesus initially saw men
like walking trees—that is, the healing wasn't finished yet (Mark
8:22–25).

   When God punished people, he also employed the nature he
had created, albeit in a supernatural way: a flood in Noah's day,
the geological destruction of Sodom, and a drought to punish
Baal worship in Ahab's day. Sometimes God used humans: the
Assyrians, who took Israel into exile, and the Persian king Cyrus,
who allowed them to return, were both sent by God to do his will
(Isa 10:5–6; 44:28). Actually, God appears to prefer doing his work
through humans (like us!) because we are the special part of his
creation who can act as his representatives.

GARDENER

Finally, we can understand why God wants to work through his
creation by imagining him as a gardener. When gardeners know
that visitors will be coming at a certain time, they will plant
bulbs so that they will be in full bloom when the visitors arrive,
and they will trim the bushes a few weeks before so that the outer
leaves recover before people see them. But when film directors

---

3. See chap. 26, "Miracles That Employ Nature."
4. See chap. 28, "Explaining the Exodus Miracles."

need to create a garden scene in a film, they'll arrange for topiary to be brought in from a garden center and for cut flowers to be pegged into the ground, and perhaps even use artificial plants. The director's method for producing a garden is totally different from that of the gardener, who has taken time to carefully create each vista that visitors will admire.

When master gardeners or groundskeepers want a fence, they plant something like a blackthorn hedge, then pleach the stems—that is, interlace them to grow into an impenetrable barrier. Gardeners could, instead, buy chain link and hammer metal posts into the ground, but they prefer to use nature. They are also likely to make seating from fallen trees and create areas of shade by growing vine bowers. God, in a similar way, uses the materials of the world he has created in order to carry out his purposes.

Sometimes this involves considerable planning and manipulation—such as setting up the geology around Sodom ready for the day when it will be destroyed. This might seem like a lot of extra work—why didn't God simply materialize the fiery brimstone in midair so that it would fall on Sodom and Gomorrah? If he had, it would have meant the angels wouldn't have had to tell Lot to hurry—the text implies there was only a limited leeway available in timing his escape (Gen 19:15–16).

If God did work independently of his creation, he would be like a gardener who buys fertilizer every year instead of planning ahead by putting aside compost. The results are the same, but the Bible describes God using nature, often with great foresight and preparation.

God, like our imaginary gardener, loves his creation, which he declared to be "very good" (Gen 1:31), so he uses it to carry out all that he wants to do. Perhaps he has to intervene rather more often than he wants to because sin has made so many unwanted

changes, but instead of starting again, he guides people and processes to produce the right results. Like a gardener who introduces ladybirds to kill aphids instead of spraying them with
insecticide, God is always looking for a more "natural" way to
perform his purposes. Why? Because he created nature and loves
to use it.

SUMMARY

- Miracles in the Bible don't involve materialization.

- Creation isn't described as instantaneous.

- Augustine imposed his own conclusion that God
  acts instantaneously.

- *Proposal*: God creates and tends his creation by
  encouraging natural progression and growth.

2

▼

God *Does* Work in the Gaps

We tend to ascribe to God only the things we don't yet understand, such as how life began—that is, the gaps in our knowledge. But there's a different kind of gap that would allow him to do anything he wished without breaking any of the observable laws of physics.

The phrase "God of the gaps" is a derogatory way to point out that our "proofs" for God tend to rely on things that science can't explain yet—with the result that God's activity appears to shrink as our knowledge grows. When we didn't understand lightning, we assumed that God sent it and that he was carrying out his judgment on anyone it struck. And when we didn't understand why harvests failed or why a couple was childless, we assumed that God was the one who sent fertility, so we had to pray that crops would grow and children would be born—otherwise they wouldn't.

When we look back at societies that worshiped storm gods such as Baal and performed fertility rites such as those around Asherah poles in Old Testament times (e.g., Judg 3:7; 1 Kgs 15:13; 18:19; 2 Kgs 23:7), we regard them as naive or credulous. This isn't because we think God isn't involved, but we realize that these things will happen according to natural causation, whether or not we pray for them.

SHRINKING GAPS

The belief that God personally directs every event has persisted even in scientifically sophisticated societies. When Benjamin Franklin invented lightning rods in 1752, most churches refused to fit them because they thought they interfered with God's ability to smite people. Dances around maypoles were still being regarded as fertility rituals even in the 1800s.[1] Now that we understand more, we generally regard lightning strikes, famines, and infertility as random evils that occur without any specific direction from God. As our knowledge has gradually increased, there are fewer and fewer unexplained events that we would previously have attributed to God. This means that we end up thinking about God's role in fewer and fewer actions—those that remain within the shrinking gaps in our understanding.

As Christians, we might assert that God *can* still send lightning and infertility as he wills—but do we really believe this? Our actions don't bear this out: When, for instance, did you last hear a prayer asking God to strike an evil person with lightning? Or a prayer asking God to stop making someone infertile or stop punishing a particular country with famine? Instead, we pray that God would *protect* people from bad weather and help them *overcome* infertility and bad harvests. This is because we regard fertility of land and people as normal, so we don't normally pray for fertility unless something goes wrong.

We no longer consider that God has given himself the job of making the sun and stars move, or showing birds where to migrate. We wouldn't think of pleading with God to bring back the sun when we reach the winter solstice—because we expect

---

1. Sir James George Frazer, writing in 1894, was still finding such customs being linked to fertility. See *The Golden Bough* (New York: Macmillan, 1894), 1:72–81 (TinyURL.com/FrazerMaypole).

that to happen without our prayers. And as weather prediction becomes better, it seems increasingly strange to pray for sunshine or rain. We now understand, as Jesus taught, that sun and rain are delivered equally to good and evil people (Matt 5:45).

HOLDING IT ALL TOGETHER

Perhaps we have lost sight of the fact that God in the Bible *does* claim to run the universe. The same verse in which Jesus says that good and bad weather arrive irrespective of whether people are good or bad also says that sun and rain are delivered by "your Father in heaven"—he makes the sun rise each day. But how literally should we take that? Does God really intervene so constantly and predictably in the world? Does Jesus personally supervise every force of gravity and atomic forces? This is certainly how some people would interpret Paul's words "in him all things hold together" (Col 1:17).

When science started making progress in the eighteenth century, a new type of religious thought became popular: deism. Deists believe that God created the world, gave it natural laws, set it running, and now merely watches its progress. In contrast, theists agree that creation runs by itself according to natural laws, but they also believe that God intervenes to influence personal affairs.

The Bible implies something similar to theism because it describes God personally interacting on specific and rare occasions in a special way, commonly called a miracle. Of course, there may be many more unseen miracles, but the implied principle is that the world runs by itself—albeit imperfectly because of the presence of sin—and God intervenes when necessary.

Does this mean that God occasionally breaks the laws of physics in order to perform his special will? Of course, this is possible, but it is also possible that God works by using his own creation within the parameters he has given it—even when performing a miracle.

A possible way for him to do this lies in the tiniest of all gaps in the universe: the quantum gaps of uncertainty in subatomic events. We will see that this allows God to do things that we normally call *impossible* but that should really be described as extremely *improbable*.

QUANTUM GAPS

The Heisenberg uncertainty principle states that the exact position and movement of a subatomic particle, such as an electron, can only be determined up to a specific built-in limitation. It is impossible to pinpoint the exact position of any particle more accurately than 10^{-35} meters. This can't be solved by making instruments more accurate. It is due to the way that particles such as an electron act like a wave or area of force, so that their position is literally uncertain. It might be in one position, or it might be in any other position within the small radius of uncertainty. This is not just a theoretical issue, because its dual nature—being both a wave and a particle at the same time—is employed in electron microscopes and GPS systems.

One consequence of this uncertainty is that we can't predict what will happen when two particles collide. When a photon (a particle of light) hits an electron inside a solar panel, it may or may not knock it off the atom it is attached to. If it does, some electricity is generated, and if not the panel will just gain a little heat. What actually happens doesn't only depend on the energy of the light or the exact type and position of the electron: even if the circumstances are exactly the same, there is still uncertainty about the outcome. We can predict that an electron will be dislodged a certain percentage of occasions, but no one can know what will happen on any one particular occasion. It is literally uncertain.

This means that if God made the light dislodge an electron on one particular occasion, no laws of physics would be broken. Of course, no one would notice one electron, but in a system where normally only 10 percent of electrons are dislodged by photons, God *could* make 50 percent of the electrons be dislodged. Suddenly the solar panel would produce five times as much electricity—which certainly could be noticed. This still would not break any laws of physics, although it would be *very* improbable; and the longer it continued, the more improbable (i.e., miraculous) it would become.

USING THE IMPROBABLE

Improbable events happen all the time—for example, when an atom of carbon-14 decays into nitrogen, which is the process by which we measure archaeological time. Carbon-14 is a rare form of carbon created by cosmic rays in the atmosphere. Plants make carbon into food for us, and about one in a trillion of those carbon atoms is carbon-14. In about fifty-seven hundred years, half of our carbon-14 will be gone—but no one can predict which atoms will have decayed and which ones will remain. Now and then, at a totally unpredictable moment, one of the neutrons in carbon-14 will split into a proton and an electron, so that the carbon atom becomes a nitrogen atom. If this carbon atom happened to be part of an important gene that prevents cancer, this could have terrible consequences.

The improbable but normal process that turns carbon-14 into nitrogen is called tunneling—an electron tunnels out through the barrier that keeps it within the neutron. This barrier is a like a wall of energy, and the bigger that wall, the less likely that the electron will escape. If the energy wall is small, this will happen often, but even if the wall is high it will still happen occasionally. It is like a sea wall that successfully keeps the town from being swamped on a stormy day, but occasionally you'll taste salt on your lips because a drop of water has made it over the wall.

Now imagine a jug of water, made of hydrogen and oxygen. It also contains some dissolved air—which will bubble off if you boil it—consisting of nitrogen, oxygen, and carbon dioxide. If some of those atoms moved out of their molecules and joined together (three nitrogen, five carbons, and nine hydrogens) and collected in the shape of a double-ringed amine, then a molecule of histamine would pop into existence. This is the chemical in bee stings that makes us reach for antihistamine cream, and it is also the chemical in red wine that is thought to give us headaches. Producing a histamine molecule in this way would be a very improbable event, though not impossible. And even if that improbable single molecule of histamine *was* produced, we certainly wouldn't notice it—so we don't have to be wary of drinking water. It is vanishingly improbable that more than one molecule would be formed, and even more massively improbable that other similar amines or other organic compounds would form in measurable quantities. However, the probability never reaches zero, so we can't call these transformations scientifically impossible.

You have probably guessed what I'm leading up to: a massive occurrence of specific quantum tunneling could turn water into wine. This has been seriously discussed by philosophers such as Alvin Plantinga and physicists such as Paul Davies.[2] They point out, in much more erudite detail, that this is so unlikely that it is nonsense to calculate a statistical probability—but it is, nevertheless, theoretically possible. So, when Jesus turned water into

---

2. See an interview with Paul Davies, "Does God Play Dice?," *Australian Broadcoasting Company* (TinyURL.com/DaviesDice), and a discussion of Plantinga's ideas by Bradley Monton in "God Acts in the Quantum World," *Oxford Studies in Philosophy of Religion* 5, no. 7 (TinyURL.com/PlantMont).

wine, it was certainly miraculous, but he didn't need to break any laws of nature to do so.

They conclude that most of the miracles of the Bible can be regarded in a similar light—as instances of extremely improbable quantum tunneling. This process enables atoms (and the objects they make up) to move virtually anywhere, and even allows one element to be changed into another.

Now, this kind of description doesn't explain away miracles. Miracles are still impossible in the sense that they are too improbable to ever occur during the lifetime of the universe—let alone at a significant moment. However, quantum tunneling means that these statistically impossible events are not scientifically *impossible*.

CHANGING THE WORLD

It turns out that God's actions might be found in gaps after all—but not in the gaps of our knowledge. God's action may be situated in the quantum gaps we can't predict or control. These tiny gaps of uncertainty can never be predicted, and although they appear to be insignificant, the tiny quantum actions within these gaps add up to the actions that our observable world is constructed from. Therefore God could, without breaking any laws of physics, change the physical world in all kinds of ways. If God controls all of these gaps at the quantum level, he would have no difficulty making any number of observable events occur in a way that is statistically improbable but not impossible—for example, producing wine from a jug of water.

Deists argue that God simply leaves his creation to run the way that he has designed it, so he doesn't need to interact with it. But several accounts in the Bible suggest that God does occasionally step in and make things happen in a miraculous way. Using the model of quantum tunneling, we see that a miracle *can*

happen when God moves his creation in unusual directions—
and that he can do this without breaking any of the physical laws
he has built into the universe. This does not mean that we have
definitely discovered the way that God interacts with the world,
but the important conclusion is that he *could* use this method.
So if God does act in quantum gaps—where no scientific instrument can detect that anything impossible has happened—the
conclusion we can come to is that something *extremely* improbable has just occurred exactly when we needed it or when he
promised it to us—that is, a miracle has happened.

SUMMARY

- Ancient people believed that every individual natural event was personally directed by God.

- God's role appears to diminish as the gaps in scientific knowledge are filled.

- Quantum tunneling allows God to direct even
  improbable events.

- *Proposal:* Miracles are extremely improbable
  events directed to occur at a predicted or helpful
  time.

3

What Are the Stars For?

The stars aren't gods (as pagans thought in Bible times), or holes in the dome of heaven (as the medieval church thought). We know they are suns, and we now know why God created so many.

How do you feel when you look up at the stars on a clear night? Overawed? Inspired? Insignificant? All those suns, many with planets, put our existence into perspective. We might be forgiven for concluding that we are unimportant, but the Bible's creation narrative encourages us to thank God for the creation he made specifically for us. However, if this universe really is made for us, it can be difficult to understand why there are so many stars—what are they there for? In the vastness of the universe, our insignificance makes us seem like an accident looking for a purpose, but modern astronomy may help us understand what the Bible tells us about stars and their purpose in God's creation.

In ancient times, when people looked at the heavens they were awed and somewhat terrified—believing they were seeing gods. It was a logical conclusion: the stars twinkle and move with apparent life, and they are clearly a long way away, so they must be huge. Also, they appear to be powerful because their movements reflect events on Earth: seasons change with the stars; the moon moves the tides; and the sun changes the weather.

In the face of this widespread belief, it is remarkable that the Israelites, and subsequently Christians, came to believe that there is only one God. One of the ways that the Bible asserts this is to say that this one God created and controls the stars. Instead of attempting to challenge the concept that the stars are gods by simply denying it, the Old Testament writers refer to them as God's "army." This is how they are described in Genesis 2:1, which says (translating word-by-word), "And he completed the heavens and the Earth and the whole army"—though most English translations use the old English word for an army: "host."

LORD OF HOSTS

Israel called their God "the LORD of hosts" because he commanded the armies of stars. The word *tsava* (translated "host") is the normal Hebrew word for an "army," so the phrase "LORD of hosts" was an excellent translation in the days of King James. Nowadays we should perhaps translate it "LORD of armies," and this is how it is translated in most non-English Bibles. For example, traditional Spanish Bibles use "JEHOVÁ de los ejércitos"— though I do like the phrase "Dios del universe," which replaces this in some modern Spanish Bibles. However, "LORD of armies" sounds rather militaristic, so English versions such as the ESV, NRSV, and NASB tend to stick with the archaic word "hosts." The NIV often uses "LORD Almighty," following a convention that started before Jesus' day in the ancient Greek translation (see the quotation of Isa 6:3 at Rev 4:8).

The title "LORD of hosts" completely changed ancient Israel's perceptions about the stars. Instead of thinking of them as gods, people in the Old Testament regarded them as part of God's workforce or entourage. Occasionally, stars were identified as angels (Pss 103:21; 148:2; Job 38:7), but never as foreign gods (though Deborah almost implied this at Judg 5:20-23). This was an amazing contrast to other nations' belief that the stars were gods.

Keeping so many Bible authors on message over hundreds of years helps to convince me of the Holy Spirit's intervention in writing Scripture. Claiming that the national deity of Israel controlled all the stars in the universe is as audacious as a hacker who claims to control all the computers on the planet. Nevertheless, this assertion won the day in Israel, and then in Christendom. Even the monotheism of Islam was inspired by the Bible, which was Muslims' holy book before the Qur'an. (The Qur'an refers to the Bible as "the Book," and Muslims still regard a printed Bible as too holy to place on the floor even for a moment.) But as well as teaching that God is in charge of the whole universe, the Bible has another implied message: humanity is at the center of the universe, surrounded by the stars.

We now know that all stars are suns like our own sun, and many have planets around them. But the road to acknowledging this was a bumpy one. Not only did it raise questions about the purpose of so many "extra" suns, but it also created new theological problems, as people found out when they started to voice their discoveries and new ideas.

LIFE ON OTHER PLANETS

In celebration of our thirtieth wedding anniversary, my wife and I rented a small apartment for a couple of weeks near the Campo de' Fiori ("field of flowers") in Rome. This beautiful piazza was witness to an ugly history. In the middle of the market square is a statue of Giordano Bruno that looks exactly like the grim hero of *Assassin's Creed* (a popular computer game). He has the same hood, the same menacing stance, and the same angry glare—which is directed across the river at the Vatican. The statue marks where Bruno was burned at the stake in 1600 for, in addition to questioning several key Christian doctrines, suggesting that the stars are actually suns that could have planets of their own.

It wasn't until nearly four hundred years later, in 1992, when the first planet was found around another star, that astronomers could be sure that Bruno was right. The Kepler space telescope later discovered another 2,662 planets around stars in our galaxy before it ran out of fuel.[1] These include an extreme variety of bodies—one consists mainly of diamond! Earth remains very special, not only because very few of these planets are potentially friendly to life, but mainly because we are adapted to this planet—this is our home.

Is there intelligent life on other planets? This suggestion got Bruno burned at the stake. He was accused of various other heresies, which he denied, but he insistently defended his book *On the Infinite Universe and Worlds*.[2] In this he describes the heavens as "the void, in which are all those worlds which contain animals and inhabitants no less than can our own Earth, since those worlds have no less virtue nor a nature different from that of our Earth."[3]

One of his heresies was saying that there may be life on other planets—but what's wrong with that? The answer is that the Bible teaches that Christ died only once to deal with all sin, in contrast to the Old Testament sacrifices, which had to be repeated constantly (Rom 6:10; Heb 7:27). If other worlds had sinners, this teaching was a problem. Would Christ's death on Earth cover them too, or does "die once" refer only to him dying as a human?

---

1. See Wikipedia, "Kepler Space Telescope" (TinyURL.com/KeplerST).

2. See Wikipedia, "Giordano Bruno" (TinyURL.com/GioBruno).

3. See Giordano Bruno, "Third Dialogue," in *On the Infinite Universe and Worlds* (Venice, 1584) (TinyURL.com/BrunoWorlds).

C. S. Lewis had an intriguing solution for this problem in his novels about life on Mars and Venus.[4] He suggested that the Earth may be different from other planets because Satan came here and corrupted humans—unlike on other planets, which never suffered the fall. This means Jesus would never have had to die on another planet to save its inhabitants from sin.

Personally, I don't see any problem with the idea that Jesus redeems other planets. Perhaps he has several forms or faces in heaven, like some angels do (Ezek 10:14; Rev 4:6–8). That way he could represent every planet he has saved. And I see no reason why we should expect the Bible to tell us about all of this, because it wasn't written to instruct us about the whole universe—only about how God wants to rescue us and how we should live.

However, whether or not Jesus redeemed other planets, this doesn't answer the question of why there are so many stars in the first place. Even though there are planets around many of them, these are mostly uninhabitable by any form of complex life that we can imagine. We have still not received any signals from intelligent life, and so far there is no evidence that even simple life has formed elsewhere. If life occurs on only our own or a few planets, why did God create all the billions of stars with no planets or dead planets?

WE NEED ALL THOSE STARS

Astronomers can now answer that question: we need a universe as large as ours in order for there to be even one planet where life can form. The atoms that make up life (such as carbon and oxygen) can only form within the core of the largest stars, and other heavier essential elements (such as iodine) can only form

---

4. See Wikipedia, "The Space Trilogy" (TinyURL.com/CSL-Space).

when those large stars explode as a supernova. This means that complex life can't form until some of the first stars have shone, collapsed, and exploded. These events fling complex elements into space, which can then coalesce to form solar systems with planets that can sustain life. A universe lighter than ours would expand too thinly, so these large stars would never form, and a universe heavier than ours would soon stop expanding and then contract before these large stars had time to explode and form the elements for life. Our universe, however, is just the right size to form life-supporting planets.[5]

Together, the Bible and science have produced a useful answer to the question of the stars. Not only do we know *what* they are, but we also know *why* they are there. Whether there is other life in the universe, this huge surplus of uninhabited star systems is still necessary. Our universe *needs* to contain a billion trillion stars—if it contained any fewer, life could never exist on even one planet.

When we stare into space, we may realize how small we are in the universe, but we are certainly not insignificant. The Bible's message is that God created this huge universe with a purpose: to support intelligent life—that is, us! The brief words "God created the heavens and the Earth" contain a far larger event than we had previously realized, and indicate how much preparation and investment was put into producing and supporting intelligent life. In other words, the vastness of empty space doesn't teach us that we are insignificant—it shows us the opposite. We are so significant to God that he created this vast universe in order to give us a home where we can live.

---

5. See Ethan Siegel, "Going Nuclear: How Stars Die," Science Blogs (TinyURL. com/HowStarsDie).

SUMMARY

- Ancient people thought the stars were gods. Medieval Christians thought they were simple lights or holes in heaven.

- The discovery that stars are suns like our own sun caused major theological problems.

- The universe needs this vast number of stars because if it contained any fewer, life could never exist on even one planet.

- *Proposal:* There are so many stars in the universe because they are needed to support life on this planet and possibly others.

4

▼

Multiverses Prove
God's Existence

Our finely tuned universe provides a valid proof for God's existence—
unless there are infinite multiverses that contain everything that can
possibly exist. However, these multiverses also provide a proof for
God—so either way, a creator exists.

I t almost seems like an anti-Christian conspiracy. Just when
God's existence appeared to be proved by the fine-tuning of
the universe, someone "invented" the multiverse—a hypothesis
that makes this finding irrelevant because at least one of these
infinite universes would be perfect for life.

It is similar to when the big bang was first discovered in
1927, and Christians celebrated its confirmation of the Bible in
showing that the universe had a dramatic beginning. Many atheists denied this discovery, especially as it was made by Georges
Lemaître, a physicist who was also an ordained priest. Fred
Hoyle tried to dismiss the idea by coining the derogatory term
"big bang"—which stuck. He came up with the "steady state"
theory, that the universe was being continuously created.[1] But

---

1. See Jim Holt, "Big Bang Theology," *Slate*, February 12, 1998 (TinyURL.
com/BigBangTheology).

this and other theories that denied the big bang were eventually disproved by Stephen Hawking and others.[2]

Of course, most scientists who are seriously investigating potential ideas in cosmology aren't interested in proving or disproving the Bible. But apologists who argue for or against Christianity certainly are interested in the theological consequences of these findings. Some atheist apologists see the multiverse as a way to avoid the conclusion that a fine-tuned universe implies a creator. From the other side, I want to point out that the opposite is actually true: a multiverse *guarantees* that a creator exists.

EXACTLY RIGHT FOR LIFE

But first, what does it mean to say the universe is fine-tuned? An increasing number of discoveries about fundamental physical constants show just how precisely this universe is suited for life. For example, if gravity were a tiny bit stronger, the universe would contain nothing but black holes; if it were a tiny bit weaker, no stars or planets could hold together. The tuning is as fine as you can imagine: an extremely tiny difference in the gravitational constant (0.00000000000000000000000000 000000000000001%) would make this universe lifeless.[3] This means that the chance of gravity being exactly right is roughly equal to someone accidentally picking out a winning lottery ball when every ball is as small as grain of sand, and the sand doesn't just fill all the deserts on the surface of this planet—the whole planet is filled with this sand, and also every other planet in our

---

2. See Stephen Hawking, "The Beginning of Time" (TinyURL.com/HawkingBeginning).

3. For a technical basis of this number, see Luke A. Barnes, "The Fine-Tuning of the Universe for Intelligent Life," *Publications of the Astronomical Society of Australia* (January 2, 2013) (TinyURL.com/GravConstant), 39–40. For a nontechnical summary of fine-tuning, see Brad Lemley, "Why Is There Life?," *Discover*, November 1, 2000 (TinyURL.com/FineTuned).

solar system. If someone traveled to the correct planet, picked the exact spot, and then drilled down—perhaps thousands of miles—before selecting this one predetermined grain of sand, they would win the kind of lottery that makes gravity just right in this universe. Gravity could be like this by chance, or it could be that a creator set it at the correct strength.

And gravity isn't the only constant that needs to be exactly right for life to exist. There is also Planck's constant, the strong nuclear force, and up to twenty-four other independent variables (the exact number isn't certain because some may turn out to be dependent on others).[4] Some of these are more finely tuned than gravity and some less, but they are all large numbers. To calculate the final improbability, you multiply all of these numbers together to arrive at a number that is so huge that it becomes meaningless to our minds.

Cosmologists have recognized the implications just as much as Christians have. Stephen Hawking says, "The values of these numbers seem to have been very finely adjusted to make possible the development of life." Martin Rees (the UK's Astronomer Royal) says that the universe appears to be "tailor-made for man."[5] The finding is astounding, and it demands an answer. Either there is a reason in physics why these numbers are all exactly perfectly tuned to enable life (and no one has any clue where to find this reason), or there is a creative genius behind it.

---

4. See Ethan Siegel, "It Takes 26 Fundamental Constants to Give Us Our Universe, but They Still Don't Give Everything," *Forbes*, August 22, 2015 (TinyURL.com/26constants).

5. For these quotes and more details, see Wikipedia, "Fine-Tuned Universe" (TinyURL.com/FineTunedWiki).

FINE-TUNING IMPLIES A CREATOR

The multiverse hypothesis appears to have rescued atheists by supposing that our universe is just one in an infinite array of universes. This multiverse includes a countless multitude of universes where some or all of the physical constants are different so they can't support life. If there is a multitude of different universes, it isn't surprising that one exists where everything is exactly tuned for supporting life, and it is easy to explain why we happen to live in it—because that's the only one we *could* live in. In this way, the multiverse hypothesis overcomes the need for a creator to fine-tune all the physical constants.

By the way, the term "hypothesis" is more accurate than "theory" in this case because there is currently no testable evidence to support the idea of a multiverse. Actually, it is difficult to think of any way in which we *could* find such evidence because, by definition, a universe is a totality of what we can perceive, so anything outside our universe should be unmeasurable and undetectable.[6]

Looking for a multiverse in the Bible is also futile because ancient Hebrew and Greek had no word for it. If such a word did exist, we'd expect to find it in Jeremiah 10:12, which lists God's domain in increasingly larger terms: "God made the land by his power; he founded the world by his wisdom and stretched out the heavens by his understanding" (adapted from the NIV). God is first praised for creating the land of Israel (or possibly all of the land masses – the word *erets* can mean either), then for creating the planet (*tevel*, which, unlike *erets*, always refers to the whole of this world), and then the largest unit, "heavens" (*shamayim*)—a

---

6. On the possibility of detecting a multiverse, see Alexander Vilenkin and Max Tegmark, "The Case for Parallel Universes," *Scientific American*, July 19, 2011 (TinyURL.com/SciAmMultiverse).

plural word that includes the sky that contains clouds and the sky that contains all the stars. This could be said to include the whole of our universe, but it couldn't be stretched to make it include other universes. Of course, this doesn't mean that we can definitely exclude multiverses from the Bible's landscape. After all, we read that "God created the heavens and the earth" (Gen 1:1), which we normally regard as shorthand for everything.

However, it is arguable that we can find fine-tuning in the Bible. God gave Job some wonderful insights into his creative work, in which he attempted to stretch Job's understanding. God told him: "I laid the earth's foundation ... marked off its dimensions ... shut up the sea behind doors. ... I fixed limits for it ... gave orders to the morning ... and showed the dawn its place" (Job 38:4–5, 8, 10, 12). If Job had spoken modern English and knew some basic science, God could have put it like this: "I fixed gravity to set the earth in orbit, measured the nuclear force to make a planet the right size, gave the moon enough mass to make tides, and set dawn's light at the right speed and luminosity." This remarkable text gets very close to describing how God fine-tuned the universe.

A MULTIVERSE IMPLIES A CREATOR

Are atheist apologists correct to conclude that a multiverse hypothesis removes the necessity for a creator? Surprisingly, the reverse is true: it turns out that a multiverse *must* contain a creator.

One curious and unintuitive aspect of a multiverse is that it includes every possible variation, so that everything that *can* exist *must* exist in at least one universe.[7] This infinite variety

_____

7. This discovery by Gottfried Wilhelm Leibniz is the basis of the powerful tool of modal logic. See Brandon C. Look, "Leibniz's Modal Metaphysics,"

includes the highly improbable mix of physical constants that are exactly tuned to support things as complex as living creatures. But it also includes a universe where an all-intelligent, all-powerful individual would exist—someone with such awesome capabilities that they could communicate with other universes and even create universes. They would be able to control the forces of physics in their created universe and design the exact mix that enables the existence of biologically based life. In other words, an infinite multiverse must contain a creator God.

I'm not suggesting that this describes the God of the Bible. My goal is only to point out that the existence of a multiverse does not disprove the existence of a creator—it implies that a creator *must* exist. In an infinite variety of universes, there must be one that contains every conceivable person or thing that we can imagine, and it is certainly possible to imagine a being who can learn to harness the power and ability to make matter into any form that they wish, including a universe such as the one we inhabit.

So if the idea of a multiverse really is a conspiracy to get rid of God, it has backfired. Of course, most multiverse hypotheses are based on serious mathematical possibilities in quantum physics or string theory, and they don't have any antitheological agenda. However, some people do use them to counter the argument that the supreme fine-tuning of our universe necessitates the existence of a creative genius.

Atheist apologists are now painted into one of two corners. If ours is the only universe, then its perfectly fine-tuned design is a huge coincidence that is very difficult to explain without a creative designer. On the other hand, if ours is one of an infinite

in *The Stanford Encyclopedia of Philosophy*, Spring 2013 ed., ed. Edward N. Zalta (TinyURL.com/LeibnizModal).

multitude of universes, then a creator who can design a universe like ours must exist somewhere within this multiverse. The existence of a creator is therefore inescapable, because it is a conclusion that arises from both of these mutually exclusive views of cosmology.

SUMMARY

- Physical constants are exactly fine-tuned to allow life.

- This is so surprising it can be regarded as a proof of creation.

- It becomes unsurprising if ours is one universe in a multiverse.

- Everything that *can* exist *must* exist in an infinite multiverse.

- **Proposal**: If there is a multiverse, it must include a being like God; and if there is no multiverse, the fine-tuning of this universe implies that God exists.

5

▾

Mathematics of Infinity
and Eternity

Infinity is an important concept in mathematics. Strangely, unlike most other branches of mathematics, it doesn't represent anything in the natural world—unless it tells us about God himself.

Mathematics isn't really a science. It is an entirely independent intellectual pursuit that just happens to reflect reality. When new branches of mathematics arise, they initially look like mere games with numbers. However, eventually they turn out to be useful and often invaluable for advancing some new area of discovery or invention. It seems that all the mathematics that we "invent" in our imagination are actually a discovery about something that already exists. For example, fractals, which require computers to explore properly, don't merely produce pretty patterns; they describe the way that plants grow— and three-dimensional fractals are found in the distribution of blood vessels in our lungs.[1]

This kind of tie between mathematics and the real world is no longer surprising. Galileo first spotted the fact that "the

---

1. See Wikipedia, "Fractal" (TinyURL.com/WikiFractal).

universe ... is written in the language of mathematics."[2] Some terms in this language are so common that they have their own symbol—such as infinity (∞), the ratio of a circle's circumference to diameter (π), the exponential growth constant (e), and the "imaginary" square root of –1 (i). We can demonstrate practical uses for most of these: π for calculating circles, e for calculating compound interest, and i to calculate the electric current needed to boil all the kettles during a World Cup halftime.[3] We might reasonably expect that every new discovery in mathematics will eventually lead us to a new understanding of some aspect of the universe—but infinity remains an exception.

IS INFINITY ABSURD?

Infinity is a mathematical necessity, but it has no practical correspondence to reality. Infinity is important in the Bible for describing the eternity of God and his infinite greatness (e.g., Exod 15:18; 1 Kgs 8:27). And infinity is implied by any system of numbers that can continue without limit. But in the world described by the sciences, there is nothing that corresponds to infinity.

We used to think that space was infinite, but the consensus now is that the matter in the universe spreads across about ninety billion light years.[4] The empty space beyond may technically be infinite, but this is a nonpractical example of infinity, because space without matter is not really anything except direction.

---

2. See Wikipedia, "The Assayer" (TinyURL.com/WikiAssayer).

3. See Chris Budd, "Complex Electricity," *Plus*, November 24, 2017 (TinyURL.com/ComplexElectricity).

4. See Chris Baranuik, "It Took Centuries, but We Now Know the Size of the Universe," BBC Earth, June 13, 2016 (TinyURL.com/SizeUniverse).

Time is also finite. For time to exist, things need to happen, to mark time. An expanding universe, such as the one we live in, will eventually cool down until no energy or movement remains. If the density of matter is high enough to make the universe collapse again into a singularity, it might then burst out in a new big bang and go through this cycle indefinitely. However, time itself still wouldn't be infinite, because there is no continuity from the universe before a big bang into the universe after a big bang. That is, there is no information or memory of anything or even a single atom that existed in the previous universe that will be present in the next. Everything literally starts again, including time.[5]

Even the concept of the infinitely small has been abandoned. All matter is made of atoms about 10^{-10} meters in diameter, which are made of quarks and gluons; even light is made of discrete units (photons), so nothing can be shaved smaller infinitely. The exception may be time, though ancient Greek philosopher Zeno (in the fifth century BC) demonstrated the absurdity of infinitely small units of time in the paradox behind the fable of the tortoise and the hare.[6] The hare gives the tortoise a head start, but he never catches up because every time the hare has reached where the tortoise was, the tortoise will have walked a little farther. As the distances get infinitely smaller, the intervals of time will become infinitely smaller too, so that the hare will never be able to catch up with the tortoise. This conclusion is clearly absurd and therefore wrong, and the simplest explanation is that there is something wrong with the concept of infinity.

---

5. See Stephen Hawking, "The Beginning of Time" (TinyURL.com/ HawkingBeginning).

6. See Wikipedia, "Zeno's Paradoxes" (TinyURL.com/ZenoPara).

A modern mathematician, David Hilbert, added a new set of paradoxes to show that the concept of infinity results in absurdity; these were based on a hotel with an infinite number of rooms (it is worth watching the animation).[7] Some mathematicians (such as Doron Zeilberger) have similar suspicions about infinite numbers. They suggest there must be a maximum number after which the next number is zero. For a brief period, when my daughter was about four years old, she though there weren't any numbers beyond sixty-three—perhaps this was a significant mathematical insight that has yet to be proven.[8]

ZERO SOLVES INFINITY

Interestingly, the number zero has an entirely different history. Whereas infinity was discussed by ancient Greek philosophers, zero wasn't discussed by scholars until about a thousand years later, by Indian mathematician Aryabhata in about AD 500. The mathematics of zero was gradually developed by others, including Brahmagupta a century later, who initially rejected it as a number, because dividing any number by zero always gave the same answer—infinity. However, zero was useful in practice, unlike infinity, so zero survived. Actually, zero had already been used as a place marker in practical calculations by merchants since Sumerian times (about 6000 BC), so in this case it seems practical applications preceded the mathematics, rather than the other way around.[9]

---

7. See the fun video by Jeff Dekofsky, "The Infinite Hotel Paradox," Ted Ed (TinyURL.com/p84db45).

8. For a detailed discussion of whether actual infinity occurs in reality, see Bradley Dowden, "The Infinite," Internet Encyclopedia of Philosophy (TinyURL.com/Real-Infinity).

9. See "The Development of Zero," 3010tangents (blog), February 23, 2015 (TinyURL.com/FindingZero).

Newton benefited from this work on zero and combined it with his new mathematics of calculus to solve Zeno's paradox. Instead of trying to calculate an infinite series of time divisions, he combined them into a single set that includes constant change. Newton also developed the mathematics of gravity, which showed that Galileo's insight was right: the universe really does run according to mathematical rules. Newton didn't conclude from this that God isn't needed to run the universe. Instead, he concluded that God created the universe in a mathematically perfect way. However, he rejected the suggestion of Leibniz that God simply wound up the universe and left it to run alone. Newton concluded: "This most beautiful system of the sun, planets, and comets, could only proceed from the counsel and dominion of an intelligent Being. ... This Being governs all things, not as the soul of the world, but as Lord over all."[10]

INFINITY IN THE BIBLE

This surprising lack of infinity in any scientific field is contrasted by the Bible, where infinity is a very important concept. However, even there it was disputed by the Sadducees, who said that there was no such thing as eternal life because the Old Testament didn't mention it. Their theological opponents, the Pharisees, did find eternity in Exodus 15:18, which said the Lord would give the Israelites a home where he "reigns for ever and ever." This text said that God was eternal, but the concept of eternal life was applied also to individual believers (Ps 52:8; 145:1; Dan 12:3). The Sadducees argued that these phrases only referred to the whole of this life. However, the Pharisees replied

---

10. Isaac Newton, *Principia* 3, discussed in Wikipedia, "Religious Views of Isaac Newton" (TinyURL.com/NewtonReligious).

that if this were so, it would only say "for ever," and the addition of "and ever" showed that it means the everlasting next life too.

This was such an important discovery for the Pharisees that they inserted the phrase from Exodus 15:18 into the start of their daily prayers. Modern Judaism is descended from the Pharisees (the Sadducees all died in the destruction of Jerusalem in AD 70), and modern practice holds a clue about the ancient usage of this phrase. When Jews say this phrase in prayer, the custom is to speak it in a semiwhisper even to this day—though no one knows why. My theory is that it wasn't in the original prayer said by both Sadducees and Pharisees. So when the Pharisees added it, they did so under their breath as a kind of rebellion. Christians also adopted the phrase "for ever and ever," and it became an important statement about the eternity of Jesus (Gal 1:5; Heb 1:8; 13:21; 1 Pet 4:11; 5:11; Rev 1:18; 4:9–10; 5:13; 11:15) and the reward of individual believers (Rev 22:5).

Perhaps mathematics and the Bible can help each other solve the conundrum that infinity is a necessary element of mathematics, and yet it has no role in practical science. If mathematics does reflect reality (as it appears to do, in a remarkable way), we might expect there to be something that does correspond to infinity in reality. We have seen that infinity is an important concept in the Bible, so could it be that God is the reality that is witnessed to by the mathematics of infinity?

The universe has intimations of infinity in both the unimaginably tiny components that make up matter and its vastness of space and time, and yet it lacks actual infinity. But if we add the factor that it was created by an infinite God, who will perpetuate elements (or persons) that belong to this universe forever, then the concept of infinity gains a role in the reality of this universe.

I don't mean that infinity is such an awesome concept that the existence of this idea proves we have been inspired by an infinite God—this was the basis of Descartes' ontological proof for the existence of God. We aren't really awed by infinity anymore, so the argument no longer works. What I mean is that infinity is an inescapable aspect of our mathematics and our thinking, and yet there is nothing corresponding to it in reality unless we acknowledge the reality of God.

Mathematics appears at times to be simply playing with numbers. But there is a remarkable correspondence between reality and the strange and complex mathematical concepts that have been discovered. It seems, then, that mathematics may be not only a silent witness to the complexity of God's creation, but a witness also to God himself.

SUMMARY

- Mathematics is a theoretical invention that happens to reflect reality.

- Even strange aspects such as imaginary numbers eventually find practical applications.

- Infinity is an exception: it has no correspondence in practical science.

- *Proposal:* Infinity describes some aspects of God but no aspects of the physical universe. This implies that God is part of the reality of the universe as described by mathematics.

6

▼

Where Does God Live?

String theory describes an eleventh dimension termed M, which is equally close to every physical point. This can help us understand God's omniscience and omnipresence.

W hen Yuri Gagarin became the first man in space in 1961, he was quoted as saying that he "didn't see God there." Actually, he certainly didn't say this in any recorded or written conversations. His friend Colonel Valentin Petrov doubted that he *would* ever have said this because he was a practicing Orthodox Christian who had baptized his daughter just before the flight. The real origin of these words was a speech by Soviet leader Nikita Khrushchev, who attributed these words to Gagarin at an antireligion rally.[1]

Even at that time, when we knew so little about the universe, few people expected that God would become visible if we simply flew above the atmosphere. And in the days when people believed that the firmament was a solid dome above the earth with holes through which we saw the light of heaven, I doubt that their view of God was simply that he lived "out there." Serious thinkers realized that the question "Where does God live?" is meaningless because God is *every*where and not *some*where. As

---

1. See Wikipedia, "Yuri Gagarin" (TinyURL.com/WikiGagarin).

ancient Greek philosopher Epimenides wrote in the sixth–seventh century BC: "In God we live and move and have our being"—which Paul cited as a starting point to explain Christian beliefs (Acts 17:28).

EVERYWHERE AND EVERYWHEN

Psalm 139 is a more extensive exploration of God's omnipresence, which says he is present at every moment of everyone's life. We usually see this psalm as a celebration of God being with us at all times and in all places. However, reading between the lines, the psalmist may not be entirely happy that God sees everything he does and knows everything he is thinking about. He says: "You hem me in behind and before. ... Where can I flee from your presence? ... If I say, 'Surely the darkness will hide me' ... darkness is as light to you" (vv. 5, 7, 11–12). Although in most translations the psalmist praises God's omnipresence as "wonderful" and "precious" (vv. 6, 17), these words could also be translated differently, as "incomprehensible" and "costly."

Another ambiguity about God's ever-present eye being either comforting or uncomfortable occurs when Zechariah speaks about the "eyes of the LORD that range throughout the earth" (Zech 4:10). This sounds as though God is concerned about us, but the phrase "the eyes of the king" was an ancient way of referring to spies, so God's watchfulness could be viewed in a more sinister way—he sees and knows more than the best secret-service agency. Most people, however, are happy with the idea that God watches us and knows all about us.

When we bring science to bear on God's omnipresence, there are two main questions we tend to ask: Where is God? and, How can he be everywhere? Years ago, if a five-year-old asked, "Where does God live?," their parents may well have answered,

"Up there." Today they are more likely to say, "In his own dimension." (And if that provokes yet more questions, they can refer their offspring to fantasy-adventure cartoons!) However, this apparently facile answer might have some truth to it—it is likely that this universe has more dimensions than we can perceive, and one of them is literally everywhere.

EXTRA DIMENSIONS

These extra dimensions are predicted by string theory. This branch of theoretical physics attempts to combine the mathematics of quantum physics (which successfully describes the movement of subatomic particles) with general relativity (which successfully links gravity with everything else). In order to encompass both of these, string theory proposes that, as well as the dimension of time and the three dimensions of space that we are all aware of, there are other dimensions we can't perceive. Its basic idea is that subatomic particles, such as electrons, are actually one-dimensional bodies, like infinitely thin pieces of string. These strings "vibrate" in various ways to produce their different characteristics, such as a negative charge.

String theory may sound strange, but it has been impressively successful in explaining a few areas we would otherwise not understand. For example, it can describe some real-world phenomena in black holes, and it helps to explain how condensed matter works in superconductors. This suggests that string theory isn't just a mathematical curiosity but might actually represent reality. In 1995 Edward Witten united five separate string theories by the addition of an eleventh dimension, which he labeled "M" for "mystery." This was the start of M-theory, which it is hoped will one day become a "theory of everything"—that is, it will accurately describe the movements and interactions of all types of matter and energy from the astro-nomical to the subatomic scale.[2]

The obvious question is: Why can't we perceive these addi-tional dimensions? After all, they aren't parallel universes—they are part of this universe. So why aren't we able to see or sense them? We don't yet know the answer, but the most likely one is that their area of influence is too small. For example, if you look at a cable from a distance, it appears to be a one-dimensional line, and you only discover that it has height and depth when you get closer. So, if these extra dimensions are very small (smaller than Planck's constant of 10^{-35}m) they will be literally beyond anything that *can* be perceived.

What does all this have to do with where God lives? The key lies in a unique property of the eleventh dimension, also known as M-space: it is in touch with every particle in the universe, so it literally extends everywhere. And yet its physical properties are such that it cannot be perceived by any human sense or by any instrument we can ever invent.

If, like me, you are among the millions of fans of author Terry Pratchett, you'll be familiar with the concept of L-Space in his Discworld novels. He worked in the nuclear industry before his novels became popular, so he knew about M-theory long before most people, and L-space is his parody of that concept. In this fictional L-space, every book in the universe is connected—which means you can wander down endless narrow corridors of bookshelves in one library and accidentally traverse connec-tions into the bookshelves of another library in a different city, country, or world before finding your way back (if you can).

---

2. For a fuller explanation see Wikipedia, "M-theory" (TinyURL.com/Wiki-M-Theory). To see the state of play at the time of writing, see the Cambridge PhD dissertation by N. B. Copland, "Aspects of M-Theory Brane Interactions and String Theory Symmetries," November 11, 2018 (TinyURL.com/Copland-M-Theory).

Having walked down actual miles of shelving within Cambridge University library, this idea sounds convincing to me!

String theory also calls the eleventh dimension the M-brane because it is the membrane that connects all the other dimensions (or "branes") to each other. I sometimes wonder whether physicists make up these names after binge drinking—particularly given the fact that they named the tiny single-point brane a p-brane. But weird names aside, we shouldn't be deflected from realizing that the mathematics of this theory is awesome—and it may well describe the reality we live in.

CLOSELY CONNECTED

M-theory may also describe how God is omnipresent and omniscient. If God is able to traverse the M-dimension, he is in touch with literally every particle in the universe at the same time. This means he is closer to each of us than we are to our own skin—in fact, he is in touch with every cell and atom in our body. And yet this doesn't mean that we are living inside God or that God is an inseparable part of us—he can still be completely independent from us. The language I'm using to describe this sounds quite theological, but it is nonetheless roughly how a physicist would describe the closeness of the M-dimension to each of us.

I'm not saying this is definitely how God's omniscience and omnipresence works out in practice in our universe—we don't yet know whether there is a M-dimension and, if there is, whether God actually does traverse it. The significant point is that it *could* allow us to describe these characteristics of God in a way that remains consistent with modern physics. This means there would not necessarily be any clash between the physicist and theologian in this area.

More importantly, M-theory gives us valuable insights into what omnipresence could mean. We don't have to accept either the Buddhist concept that God is omnipresent because we live inside him or the pantheist concept that God is omnipresent because he infuses everything. M-theory provides a way that a holy God can be intimately in touch with the whole of his creation while also remaining entirely separate from it. When we accept Jesus' forgiveness of sins, God *can* live inside us by his Holy Spirit; but even before that, he can know about every chemical reaction inside us, and be alongside each atom in our body, without ever being part of us. Via the M-dimension, God can remain separate from his creation while at the same time being in touch with every particle of it.

This scientific theory gives us concepts and language by which we can speak about God's presence with us and knowledge of us which is just as personal as that found in Psalm 139. But it still doesn't remove the ambivalence in my mind about whether God's constant eye on me is comforting or disconcerting.

SUMMARY

- Even ancient cultures concluded that God is everywhere, not just in heaven.

- String theory implies an eleventh dimension named M for M-brane or "membrane."

- This M-brane links every other dimension and is close to every particle in the universe.

- **Proposal:** God can traverse the M-dimension, which makes him omnipresent and omniscient.

Section 2

▾

The Earth

7

▼

The Problem with Galileo

*The church rejected Galileo because he contradicted the Bible—
though actually he only rejected its interpretation of the Bible. How
can we tell when the Bible is speaking metaphorically and when it is
trying to teach us scientific facts?*

Galileo Galilei (1564–1642) was the Richard Dawkins of his
time. Like Dawkins, he produced extremely well-written
books based on his acknowledged expertise in a specific area.
And in the same way as Dawkins, he used his communication
skills to write on subjects outside his area of expertise in order
to attack the established teaching of the church in a derogatory
and condescending manner. Both men did this in a way designed
to amuse their readers and exasperate their critics. As a result,
we remember Galileo for his disputes with the Inquisition and
forget the intricate mathematics that earned him a professorship
in Pisa and Padua. Similarly, we tend to forget Dawkins' revolu-
tionary work on gene-pool selection because of the shadow cast
by works such as *The God Delusion*.

Looking back at Galileo's discoveries, everyone agrees that
the church could have reacted better. But how were they to
know that he was right and their interpretation of the Bible
was wrong?

The idea that the earth and other planets revolve around the sun was proved by Nicolaus Copernicus, who (sensibly!) published his work just before he died in 1543. Fifty years later, Galileo was appointed to teach mathematics in Padua and was studying Copernicus' work.[1] The church hadn't minded too much when Copernicus proved by complex mathematics that the sun and planets didn't all revolve around the earth. But Galileo was a populist and a showman—and, worse still, he invented a telescope by which anyone could see that he was right.

In 1610 Galileo published a book with drawings of what he could see through his telescope, including pictures of the moons of Jupiter disappearing behind the planet and then appearing again.[2] He invited famous and influential people to come see this for themselves, so even those who had no interest in astronomy shared what they had seen at social gatherings. Copernicus had contradicted the accepted theory that everything revolves around the earth, but Galileo transformed this into an observable fact—a fact that was deemed heretical.

These new ideas sounded wild and unbelievable, as well as heretical. They claimed that rather than being stationary, the earth is traveling at 67,000 miles per hour around the sun, along with the other planets. Later we discovered that the band of stars called the Milky Way is our local galaxy and that some of the faint stars that we can see are actually distant galaxies made up of millions of stars. The planet Earth isn't at the center of anything.

This was a terrible moment from which the church hasn't really recovered. Instead of using scientific observations to help

---

1. In 1597 Galileo wrote to Johannes Kepler that he had agreed with Copernicus' views for some years. See "Brief Biography of Johannes Kepler" (TinyURL. com/J-KeplerBio).

2. See Wikipedia, "Sidereus Nuncius" (TinyURL.com/Nuncius).

interpret the Bible, the church simply decided that its traditional understanding was correct—even if calculations and their own eyes disagreed.

INTERPRETING THE BIBLE

In the church's defense, the Bible clearly does say that the Earth stands still: "The world is firmly established, it cannot be moved"; "He set the earth on its foundations; it can never be moved" (Pss 96:10; 104:5). It also says that the Earth stands on pillars: "He shakes the earth from its place and makes its pillars tremble"; "When the earth and all its people quake, it is I who hold its pillars firm" (Job 9:6; Ps 75:3). It also says that the sun moves: "The sun rises and the sun sets, and hurries back to where it rises"; "It rises at one end of the heavens and makes its circuit to the other" (Eccl 1:5; Ps 19:6).

We could approach these texts in a number of different ways:

1. We could say that they are true from a particular perspective, in that relative to us the Earth stands still and the sun moves around us.

2. We could regard them as merely figures of speech, so we shouldn't infer anything literal from them. After all, we still speak about "sunrise" without meaning that the sun is below the horizon and actually rises above it.

3. We could agree that the ancient authors were reflecting their own beliefs about the sun moving around the Earth and that they were merely using this as an illustration of God's greatness; neither they, nor God, who inspired them, expected us to infer anything about astronomy from this imagery.

4. We could declare that anything stated in Scripture is literally true, whatever the subject matter or genre. So if other facts indicate something different, it is those facts that we need to question, not the Bible.

I like the second option—that this was simply a figure of speech. I also have a lot of sympathy for the third option—that the Bible shouldn't be expected to make revelations about matters outside its message. The first option is what I normally look for first when interpreting or translating a text—that is, to assume that the words mean what they say, but that they are not the way we would put it if we were saying it today. In other words, the Bible speaks about the sun moving around the Earth because that was how everyone described it—and how we ourselves speak about it when we aren't attempting to be scientifically accurate. Even the concept of pillars under the earth can be understood in this way. At first it appears to be utterly at odds with the reality of a sphere moving through space. However, these passages are not speaking about the planet being shaken and quaking—they are speaking about earthquakes and about the assurance that the ground won't totally topple because the foundations are sufficiently secure (see the context at Job 9:6; Ps 75:3).

THE CHURCH'S MISTAKE

As you can see, I have stated the options in the order I regard the most useful. The fourth isn't an option at all—it is a mistake. And it is the mistake that the church made with regard to Galileo's discovery. They assumed that their interpretation was the only possible interpretation. However, I don't think we can blame them because this is something we all do from time to time. We need to distinguish between *what the text tells us* and *what we impose on the text*. When the Bible appears to teach us facts about the sciences, we have to allow that this may be metaphorical. Like any good scientist, we have to investigate to find out whether something agrees with reality before we can decide which interpretation is correct.

The church declared that anything except its own interpretation of these texts was heresy. Cardinal Bellarmine (whose views defined the official position) at first took a sensible stance, arguing that there was not yet any physical evidence that the Earth moved around the sun. Galileo responded to this by publishing his work on the tides, which showed they were physical evidence that the moon moves around the Earth. If he had stopped there, he might have been left alone, but he published other works in which he made fun of several influential people, including Pope Urban VIII, whose words he put into the mouth of a fictional character called Simplicio ("simpleton").[3]

Catholics were not the only ones to reject these ideas out of hand. Calvin said that those who asserted that "the earth moves and turns" were motivated by "a spirit of bitterness, contradiction, and faultfinding ... to pervert the order of nature."[4] And Luther said, commenting on Genesis 1:6, "We Christians must, therefore, be different from the philosophers in the way we think about the causes of these things. And if some are beyond our comprehension (like those before us concerning the waters above the heavens), we must believe them rather than wickedly deny them or presumptuously interpret them in conformity

---

3. In his *Dialogue Concerning the Two Chief World Systems*. See Wikipedia, "Galileo Galilei" (TinyURL.com/WikiGalileo).

4. John Calvin, *Sermon 8 on 1 Corinthians*, 677, cited in William J. Bouwsma, *John Calvin: A Sixteenth Century Portrait* (Oxford: Oxford University Press, 1988), 72.

with our understanding." Later, commenting on Genesis 1:14, he added, "The stars ... are fastened to the firmament like globes of fire, to shed light at night."[5] Of course, Luther was writing before Copernicus, and Calvin was writing between the time of Copernicus and Galileo, so neither of them knew there could be actual evidence that supports these ideas. However, what they said implies that they considered physical sciences to be inferior to Scripture and that any evidence that might be found should be suspected as mere "faultfinding" or "wicked denials" of the truth.

Nevertheless, I have great sympathy for preachers such as Calvin and Luther, even though they made statements we might regard as laughable today. You have to scour their voluminous writings to find comments on scientific or mathematical matters such as these because they didn't spend time writing about things they didn't understand. They weren't really interested in such topics—they were far more concerned with the overarching message of Scripture. In addition, there was very little information at the time about these subjects, and books were expensive and rare. For Calvin to make comments about Copernican thinking is as surprising as a modern preacher having an opinion on epigenetic inheritance. In other words, I am amazed that Calvin was as well informed as he was about this recent and abstruse area of mathematical research, and I'm not too surprised that he didn't understand it.

FLAT EARTH

Surprisingly, some people still reject the idea that the Earth orbits the sun, that the Earth spins, or that the Earth is round.

---

5. Martin Luther, *Luther's Works*, vol. 1, *Lectures on Genesis: Chapters 1–5*, ed. Jaroslav Pelikan (St. Louis: Concordia, 1999), 30, 42.

They assert that the truth of the Bible should always triumph over scientific theories. In their view, the Bible clearly speaks of the sun traveling across the surface of the Earth, so this must be accepted as correct, and all other facts must fall into place around this truth. They reject what they call the "Copernican Deception" and point out that we should "question everything."[6] I like the policy of questioning every theory, but it requires a lot more work to do this properly than that employed by such believers. Questioning theories is what all scientists do, because they all long to discover something new that will overturn the accepted consensus and make themselves famous. But I doubt that anyone will overturn the theory of gravity in the near future.

Church leaders who examined Galileo should also have examined their beliefs. They should have asked: "Are we defending the Bible, or are we defending our interpretation of the Bible?" However, no one likes to admit they are wrong, and most people like to carry on thinking and teaching the same way they have always done. What the Inquisition lacked wasn't knowledge (we can never know everything) but humility and a thirst for knowledge. We can assert that the Bible is unassailably true, but we should never claim that our interpretation of the Bible is unassailable too.

6. See Fair Education Foundation, "Exposing the Copernican Deception," Fixed Earth (TinyURL.com/FixedEarth); Nicklas Arthur, "Flat Earth or Spherical Earth, What Does the Bible Say," Cross the Border (TinyURL.com/Flat-Sphere).

SUMMARY

- Mathematics and astronomy proved the earth moves around the sun.

- Catholic and Protestant theologians rejected this too hastily.

- All Christians now agree that the Bible supports this scientific finding.

- *Proposal:* When a text has more than one possible interpretation, science can help us decide between them.

8

▾

Six Snapshots of Creation

If you were God, how would you describe geological history to the author of Genesis? One way is to present it as six days in the life of the Earth. When we examine the text, this interpretation actually fits more literally than one-week creation.

The text of Genesis 1 has become a liability for many Christians, especially in certain professions. In America (where 38 percent of the population believes in one-week creation),[1] some seminary teachers have been dismissed for publicly supporting evolution in Genesis. The opposite happens in the UK, where even two-thirds of Evangelical Alliance members reject one-week creation.[2] I'm conscious that my own employment prospects may be reduced on both sides of the Atlantic by the following, because I want to resurrect a minority view that supports a very literal seven-day interpretation *and* four-billion-year evolution.

The view is inspired by P. J. Wiseman, the father of famous Bible archaeologist Donald Wiseman. He wrote *Creation Revealed in Six Days* (1948), in which he compared the account of the

---

1. See Art Swift, "In U.S., Belief in Creationist View of Humans at New Low," Gallup, May 22, 2017 (TinyURL.com/GallupCreationism).

2. See Evangelical Alliance, "Science, Creation and Evolution" (TinyURL.com/EAUK-Science).

six-day creation to narratives in Akkadian literature.[3] From this he concluded that Genesis wasn't describing God's work as lasting for six days, but that God taught Moses about it for six days and that Moses wrote a summary of what he had learned each day. My view is slightly different: I think the summary itself is what was revealed to the author.

This proposal suggests that Genesis 1 is, in effect, God's description of how he created the Earth—we could refer to it as "six days in the life of the Earth." God did not present a long, complex history of everything that happened. Instead, he gives us six snapshots of what things were like at six stages—that is, on six literal days he picked from among the billions of years during which he worked.

A DAY IN THE LIFE

Imagine you are God. How would you explain the history of the Earth to Moses' generation? They were just as intelligent as us, but in many areas they had far less knowledge and vocabulary than we do. They could probably name more stars and plants than most of us can, but they knew nothing about light years or genetics. One popular technique beloved by documentary journalists is to pick a few significant points in a complex process and present what was happening on those days, from morning to evening, from the point of view of someone who was there observing it.[4]

For example, if you wanted to teach someone about the establishment of Israel, you could outline the history by looking at three days: when God parted the Red Sea, when he brought

---

3. For the full text, see P. J. Wiseman, *Creation Revealed In Six Days* (Marshall, Morgan & Scott, 1948) (TinyURL.com/PJWiseman).

4. For example, "8 Days That Made Rome," a TV series on the history of Rome by Bettany Hughes (TinyURL.com/8DaysMadeRome).

down the walls of Jericho, and when he caused Cyrus to release the Israelites from exile. For each day, you could view it through the eyes of someone living at the time and describe what they saw. Could God have chosen this method? When we reread Genesis 1, this interpretation works rather well.

1. *God ... separated the light from the darkness. God called the light "day," and the darkness he called "night."*

The first day that God picked out to illustrate the story of the Earth is one where there was nothing to see except some light that had started to shine during the daytime. When the planet was still a swirling mass of dust, with a core starting to solidify, an imaginary observer looking up from the surface would have seen nothing. But as the matter gradually compacted into a planet, the swirling clouds of particles thinned sufficiently to let some sunlight through. This observer still couldn't have seen the sun—it was less visible than on the cloudiest day we ever experience. God picked, as the first day in the history of the Earth, the day on which some sunlight finally penetrated that dense cloud and brought light to the surface, a momentous event for the planet.

2. *God made the vault and separated the water under the vault from the water above it. ... God called the vault "sky."*

The second day is much later: things were now cool enough for some water to become liquid. This means that our imaginary observer could have seen that some water was in the atmosphere and some was on the ground. The atmosphere (the "sky" as we know it), was starting to form, though it was still very different from today. It was so full of water vapor that it was like a perpetual, thick fog that continued to obscure the sun—though each morning the light was able to penetrate a little more than before. This means there was energy for microscopic life to start forming.

3. *"Let dry ground appear."* ... *And the gathered waters he called "seas." "Let the land produce vegetation: seed-bearing plants and trees on the land that bear fruit with seed in it, according to their various kinds."*

Next, God picked a day when land had started appearing, separate from the oceans. Our imaginary observer would presumably have been seeing volcanoes erupting through the water and laying down magma to form land, or perhaps seeing where tectonic plates had collided to form higher areas. Some of the land that was visible on this day had been there for some time because it was already covered with plants—or possibly God was stating that this *would* happen. The sky was full of volcanic ash, and the atmosphere was still very humid and cloudy, so the sun and the other heavenly bodies were still not visible as distinct entities, though there was plenty of sunlight for the plants.

4. *"Let there be lights ... to mark sacred times, and days and years" ...* —*the greater light to govern the day and the lesser light to govern the night. He also made the stars.*

The fourth day occurred in a period after the plants had transformed the atmosphere from a vapor-filled hothouse to a clear sky with individual clouds. Between the clouds, our observer could now have seen the individual sources of light for the first time, both in the day and the night. The sun, moon, and stars had been there since God "created the heavens and the Earth" in verse 1, but they wouldn't have been visible as physical entities to an observer on earth until the atmosphere cleared sufficiently. The reduced cloud cover also allowed the seasons to assert themselves because there was more cooling in winter and heating in summer.

5. *God created the great creatures of the sea and every living thing with which the water teems and that moves about in it, according to their kinds, and every winged bird. ... God blessed them and said, "Be fruitful and increase in number."*

For his fifth day, God selected a typical day when animals had become abundant in the sea and air, though there weren't yet any large animals visible on the land. It is clear from the fossil record that life started as bacteria on land as well as in the waters, but larger creatures developed first in the water. So our imaginary observer wouldn't have been delivering a definitive report, stating that they had analyzed the land surfaces and found no life, but a report saying that they had observed life in the sea and air without observing any land creatures. Of course, many of those flying creatures set down among the dense vegetation on the land, but this didn't make them land creatures.

6. *"Let the land produce living creatures ... the livestock, the creatures that move along the ground, and the wild animals, each according to its kind." And ... God created mankind in his own image.*

And finally God chose a day when the big animals had arrived. These weren't the first land animals, because the dinosaurs and others had already come and gone since the "fifth" day in this brief history of the Earth. However, this particular day was very special because the first human was about to arrive on the scene. Lots of other animals were already present—the wild animals and the predecessors of livestock, which would be domesticated by generations of breeding. Portraying humans as the final object of creation may indicate they were the goal of all that preceded, or it may merely indicate that they arrived later than most other creatures—or, most likely, both. This day is the start of the whole story of the Bible.

> 7.   *God had finished ... so on the seventh day he rested from all his work.*

This is a sample day in the future of this planet, because Jesus said (when accused of working on the Sabbath): "My Father is always at his work to this very day, and I too am working" (John 5:17). In some senses, God's rest (and our rest) has started, but in other ways, God's Sabbath rest is waiting for us after all the struggles with evil are over (Heb 4:1–11). In the meantime, we copy the week of six days' work and one day rest, based on the way that God describes his own activity.

This Bible chapter can, of course, be interpreted in more than one way, though this interpretation is my favorite. I especially like the way it reflects the literal text, with six literal days, each of which have a morning and evening. These were literal mornings and evenings because the sun already existed—it was just obscured from the observer by the dense atmosphere.

DIFFICULTIES AND SOLUTIONS

There doesn't need to be any major conflict between science and the Genesis account. The order of events in Genesis is remarkably similar to what science has inferred by investigating the record left in fossils and in the history preserved in the DNA of living animals. The development of living things starts with plants, then animals in water, and then in air and on land. The animals in day six include the animals that developed last: wild animals, livestock, and ultimately humanity.

There is a possible difficulty in verse 20 with regard to the "winged birds" on day five, because birds developed from the winged dinosaurs, long after large animals had colonized the land. We wouldn't expect to see birds till the sixth day, along with the mammals. However, the Hebrew simply says "winged [things]" (*oph*), which often means "birds" but can also refer to "winged insects," for example, in Leviticus 11:21, 23. Insects were among the first animals to appear—as early as the Devonian period, when the sea was teeming with life and the land was still dominated by the dense plants that became coal—that is, at day five.

Another possible problem concerns the moon. If the moon was created on the fourth day, we can't explain what we have found on the moon: our astronauts brought back rocks from the moon that are essentially Earth rocks. It turns out that the material that makes up the moon isn't just similar to the Earth's crust—it is Earth's crust. The explanation is that a roving planet the size of Mars crashed into our planet long before life started, and the impact melted both bodies so they fused to become the Earth. The initial impact threw a lot of the surface of our planet into orbit where it solidified as the moon. On the Earth, the heavy metals of both bodies sank to form the iron core, leaving the remains of the lighter crust at the surface.

This event helped to make earth uniquely suitable for life. It provided a larger iron core than normal and a thinner crust—because we gained the core of the other planet, and much of the Earth's crust now makes up the moon. This iron core gives the Earth a strong magnetic field, which shields us from the cosmic rays that would otherwise kill any life unless it is underground.

The thin crust allows for tectonic movements and volcanoes, which bring precious heavy metals to the surface, where they are needed for life—and also for making things such as nails and phones. Most of that volcanic activity is now over, so we can reap the benefits in peace.

If the moon was first *seen* on the fourth day, this isn't a problem. That is, the moon already existed—its history is included in verse 1, when God "created the heavens." However, it was hidden from view by the dense, permanent clouds of water and volcanic dust that cleared by the fourth day. The stars would create a similar problem if they weren't created until the fourth day, because there are good reasons why the stars had to exist long before the Earth for life to be possible at all.[5]

A popular view is that "day" meant a very long "period of time," lasting millions of years, because although the Hebrew word *yom* normally refers to a period of twenty-four hours, it can also refer to a undefined period of time such as "the day of the Lord." However, in that case, the "evening and morning" would be mere rhetorical flourishes. The other popular view is that these are consecutive days in a one-week creation. But then there would be only four literal evenings and mornings. The first three would be metaphorical, as the only source of light would be God himself—because the sun isn't created till the fourth "day."

The creation account includes some insights that could not have been predicted by early generations. Genesis implies there was once a single land mass because it says that the waters were "gathered to one place." We now know that the ocean once surrounded the single landmass of Pangaea before the continents divided.[6] Genesis is also clear on the fact that life comes only

---

5. See chap. 3, "What Are the Stars For?"
6. See Wikipedia, "Pangaea" (TinyURL.com/WikiPangaea).

from life because everything divides "according to its kind" (Gen 1:11, 12, 21, 24–27). This is opposite from the theory of spontaneous generation of life, which says flies, vermin, and certain plants can arise spontaneously from garbage. This theory was generally accepted till the seventeenth century.[7]

Debates about the interpretation of Genesis 1 will continue and certainly won't be settled in this short chapter. My aim is not to state exactly what the chapter did mean, but to show that the chapter *can* agree with what scientists have discovered about this world. In eternity we'll probably find that no one has grasped the full truth, but the underlying message of the chapter is overwhelmingly loud and clear: God made everything, and we are his creation.

DOES IT MATTER?

Does it matter how long God took to make the Earth (see chap. 10)? I think it does, because the answer tells us something about God. If he made this planet in a week, then he has given it an appearance of history—which seems deceptive. He would have made coal shaped like trees that had never stood, and bones of dinosaurs and other fossils that had never lived. When he made the stars, he would have included the light beams that had apparently been traveling toward us for millions of years. Those beams show events millions of years ago, such as stars collapsing into black holes. Of course, if the stars and their light beams were made only a few thousand years ago, they are showing events that never really happened.

---

7. See Wikipedia, "Spontaneous Generation" (TinyURL.com/SpontGeneration).

This is called the omphalos hypothesis and has a long and respectable history.[8] It conjectures that when God created the Earth, he laid rock strata in an order that suggests a long geological history, with ancient bedrock lower than sedimentary rocks, making chalk appear to be made from sea creatures millions of years ago. He would have given the various rocks specific amounts of the radioactive decay that they would have if the earth had been forming for millions of years. All this is possible, but personally I can't envisage that God would set out to deceive us in such a calculating way and in such minute detail.

More important than this, however, is the message of the text itself. We aren't told how long creation took, but our debate about this has obscured what we *are* told. The creation account presents this living planet as a marvelous tribute to the greatness of God and his love for us, his creation, for which he has a plan and a purpose. This purpose is something that science can never discover, so it was important for God to reveal it in the Bible. The details of *how* God made our planet didn't need to be revealed by God—it could wait till we worked it out for ourselves from clues found in the rocks.

The sadness, for me, is that the debate itself has turned people away from the Bible. Some people have insisted on sticking to a particular interpretation that implies that either the Bible or countless scientific studies have got it all wrong. Instead, I'd prefer to acknowledge that some human interpretations of the Bible may be wrong and let science inform us while we look at the text again. We can then see that the discoveries of science are a wonderful confirmation of what is recorded in Genesis 1.

---

8. See Wikipedia, "Omphalos Hypothesis" (TinyURL.com/OmphalosHypothesis).

This would help many more people to accept the real message of this chapter: that God created us and loves us.

SUMMARY

- Genesis 1 can describe six literal days selected from the history of the earth.

- This implies that the sun became visible by day four, having been created before day one.

- Other interpretations regard the days as long eras or as consecutive days in one week.

- The one-week interpretation entails a metaphorical "evening and morning" before the sun is created in day four.

- *Proposal:* When a literal interpretation of the text coheres with science, we should opt for that.

9

▼

Everyone Believes in Evolution

Young-earth interpretations say that the thousands of species res-cued by Noah became the millions we see now. They say that species changed much faster at that time, while others say they always change slowly. Can we conclude which theory is wrong?

Christians who reject the theory of evolution by random mutation over billions of years don't actually reject evolution itself. Although they often avoid using the term "evolution," they agree that one species can produce many other new species, but by a much faster method than random mutation. This is the conclusion of organizations such as the Institute for Creation Research and others.[1] It is good news, because it means that all Christians can agree to praise God for the process of evolution—an amazing aspect of creation!

Young-earth theories are based on interpreting the six "days" in Genesis as consecutive short periods and regarding a global flood as the cause of worldwide geological upheaval. This means

---

1. See Institute for Creation Research, "Speciation and the Animals on the Ark" (TinyURL.com/ArkSpecies); Answers in Genesis, "How Could Noah Fit the Animals on the Ark and Care for Them?" (TinyURL.com/ArkNumbers); Creation. com, " How Did All the Animals Fit on Noah's Ark?" (TinyURL.com/ArkRoom); Genesis Apologetics, "Noah's Flood: How Could All the Animals Fit on the Ark?" (TinyURL.com/FitOnArk).

that all land animals are descended from those that were rescued by Noah, and Noah's ark could only have carried thousands of species at the most, not the millions we find on the planet today. The solution commonly proposed for this is that the word "kind" in Genesis (see 1:24; 6:20; etc.) does not mean "species" but something similar to a biologist's "genus"—a group that may contain just a couple or sometimes hundreds of similar species. That is, God created animals and plants with the potential to form new, related species, though within the constraints of their "kind." This process would have to occur very quickly; having done so, there would be no need to continue diversifying, so that creatures today produce young who are always of the same species.

LIONS AND BEARS

For example, the genus *Felidae* includes lions, cheetahs, and domestic cats, so Noah would not need to take on board all these species, but just a pair of one of them. (For his sake, I hope that the ancestral "kind" of *Felidae* was something like a domestic cat!) Similarly, he would only need to take one pair of toads and one pair of bears because after the flood they would produce natterjack toads, giant cane toads, brown bears, polar bears, and about 160 more species of toads and bears that exist today.[2]

So, surprisingly, all Christians agree that new species can develop over time. The main differences concern the speed and the process by which these changes occur. Young-earth theories reject the mechanism of random mutation—that is, the minor genetic changes that result in isolated populations becoming gradually different from each other. Instead, they assume that the "kinds" God created already contained all the genes that were

---

2. See Answers in Genesis, "No Kind Left Behind" (TinyURL.com/ArkKinds).

needed for later differentiation, so that the new species can arise very quickly.

For example, the MC1R gene determines red hair in humans and other aspects of hair color in dogs. The two dogs in the ark could, between them, carry four varieties of the same gene (technically known as alleles)—one on each pair of chromosomes. In dogs today there are actually five varieties,[3] so one of them must have occurred later as a mutation. Young-earth theories don't accept that a new species can arise through mutations, but they agree that occasional random mutations occur that may cause minor changes like this.

Intelligent design is a hybrid theory that agrees evolution can occur very quickly (like the young-earth theory requires after Noah's flood), though instances of this faster evolution could have occurred millions of years ago. In particular, the start of the Cambrian period (six hundred million years ago) left a fossil record with dramatically more variety than just a few million years previously.[4] The mechanism during these periods of faster evolution (sometimes called macroevolution) is still unknown, and some Christians theorize that on these occasions God stepped in to provide extra genetic input.

Therefore, everyone accepts that new species arose and that genetic changes are still happening; they only disagree about the mechanism and how fast it occurred. We know that modern wheats are nothing like the grass plants they were bred from, and farmers are aware that selecting seeds from the strongest plants will likely produce a superior crop next year. Similarly,

3. See DogGenetics.co.uk, "The E Series" (TinyURL.com/DogFaces).

4. See, e.g., an article by Günter Bechly, a paleontologist who came to this position as a non-Christian: "Ignoring Other Research, New Study Explains (Away) the Origin of New Body Plans," *Evolution News* (TinyURL.com/BechlyMeyer).

everyone can understand that modern antelopes are fast because they are all descended from those antelopes that didn't fall behind in the chase and get eaten. Elephants in Mozambique will soon have no tusks because those few mutant individuals that were born without tusks now have many more children than those that have been killed for their tusks.[5]

The core dispute is therefore not about *whether* species can change, but *how fast* and by what mechanism. If the process took billions of years, the mechanism can be random mutation—the same process by which elephants are slowly losing their tusks. But if the process was completed in a few centuries following Noah's flood, then it used a far faster mechanism, which we cannot see anywhere because it no longer occurs.

PRAISING GOD FOR EVOLUTION

While the arguments and debates about evolution continue unabated, it seems that we have forgotten to praise God for his creation of evolution. This enables animals and plants to adapt themselves and to thrive in completely different ways when there is a change in the environment.

Evolution results in all kinds of unique and fascinating characteristics. Peacocks look glorious because peahens pick the suitor with the best plumage. Migrating birds are so good at finding their way back home because they are descended from those that got back quickly and started mating first, so that they had more descendants—who inherited their navigational skills. Scientists recently discovered how the golden-winged warbler is able to predict and escape tornados: they can hear

---

5. See Dina Fine Maron, "Elephants Are Evolving to Lose Their Tusks, under Poaching Pressure," *National Geographic* (TinyURL.com/TusksLost).

the subsonic frequencies of the developing wind patterns.[6] Once this trait occurs, it is likely to spread because those that escape from incoming tornadoes have more offspring. Who would have thought that birds (who communicate in high-pitched tweets) would develop subsonic hearing?

Problems remain with whichever theory we propose. For example, if subsonic hearing developed in the golden-winged warbler by random mutation, what was its usefulness when it was half-developed? On the other hand, if it was part of God's inherent design, why didn't he give that ability to other birds—and to humans? More research is needed by everyone, and it is important to be honest and open to what nature teaches us, rather than prejudging the issue on the basis of our Bible interpretation.

Whether we believe in a young Earth or an old Earth, we can praise God for equipping living things with this built-in mechanism to produce new designs in response to new needs and opportunities. It is much more powerful and flexible than a fixed blueprint.

The power of evolution has now been harnessed by building it into robot programming.[7] With fixed programming, robots can greet people by name (using face recognition) and give verbal responses to simple questions (e.g., "Where is … ?"). But even if we gave these robots really clever software, they would be unable to improve much because they couldn't come up with innovative ideas. Now, however, evolutionary development is built into some robot software. Random changes are allowed to deliberately occur in their programming that can be deleted if

---

6. See Carrie Arnold, "Birds May Have Sensed Severe Storms Days in Advance," *National Geographic* (TinyURL.com/StormWarblers).

7. See Wikipedia, "Evolutionary Algorithm" (TinyURL.com/EvoAlgo).

they are useless. But if any tiny improvement is detected, the change is automatically adopted and randomly changed further. As the process is repeated, more and more improvements are gradually made. All this occurs without human help. Some such robots even invented a simple language for speaking to each other, and the neural net behind Google Translate has invented its own intermediary language to help it understand human languages.[8] Evolution is the most powerful design method available ... and we didn't invent it.

Personally, I praise God for evolution, which I regard as an amazing aspect of his wonderful creation. It is a remarkable process, invented by an awesome God, that enables life to constantly adapt to all the variety found in our world. And if God used that process to craft my body, then I'm proud to be a result of it.

SUMMARY

- Even young-earth theories require evolution to form six million species from the thousands rescued in the ark.

- Evolution still helps species adapt to new environments or new dangers.

- There are still questions about the mechanism, especially for the fast evolution required after a worldwide flood.

- **Proposal:** Instead of arguing about whether evolution happens, the important question is whether it was previously faster than it is now.

---

8. See BBC News, "Robots Develop Language to 'Talk' to Each Other" (TinyURL.com/TalkRobot); Sam Wong, "Google Translate AI Invents Its Own Language to Translate With," *New Scientist* (TinyURL.com/TranslateNeuralNet).

10

▼

How Long Did Creation Take?

Does it matter whether God took billions of years or one week? Do fossils and genetic family trees point to real history or an apparent history that God hid for us to find? The answer affects how we think about God.

All Christians agree that the origin of life is unexplained by science. Actually, all scientists agree with this too—though most would say that partial explanations exist and they expect that a detailed explanation will be found eventually. However, many experts (including Richard Dawkins) conclude that the origin of life is so improbable that it will never be repeated.[1] Dawkins says that life clearly started only once because all life on earth appears to be related, and we haven't yet found life elsewhere in the universe despite analyzing signals from space for decades.

The major question that divides Christians is how long God took over his creation. The text allows for various interpretations:

---

1. Hear Dawkins at BBC *In Our Time*, "The Origins of Life" (TinyURL.com/DawkinsBBC).

- The whole process in Genesis 1 could have taken one week.

- Creation of "the heavens and the earth" in verse 1 could have taken billions of years, with one week of special creation at the end.

- The "days" of creation could each have consisted of long periods of time.

- These six days could be a sample selected from throughout the long history of the earth.

Does it matter? The fundamental message of Genesis 1 is that God is the only creator and that humans are (according to this account) the pinnacle of this process. This message can be appreciated whichever of these interpretations are applied. However, there are nuances and details of the text that give further clues about the actual process. Also, these different interpretations have consequences for how we regard God: surely he didn't plant evidence for a long process in order to create doubt.

TAKING THE TEXT SERIOUSLY

Genesis 1 describes God working in potentially three different ways. He "created" things, "made" other things, and also "let" things happen. It is possible, of course, that the author is merely using stylistic variation so that the reader doesn't get bored with repetition—though this seems unlikely given all the other repetition within the chapter. It is therefore likely that these distinctions express three different aspects of how God works.

First, he "creates" things—Hebrew *bara*, that is, to bring something entirely new into existence. This word is used when:

- matter is created (v. 1)

- the first animal is created (v. 21)—that is, the first "soul"

- the first human being is created (v. 27)—that is, the first "spirit"

Second, Genesis says that God "makes" things—Hebrew *asah*, that is, to fashion from something that already exists. This word is used when:

- the sky is made by separating the clouds from the waters below (v. 7)

- the larger animals are made (v. 25)

- humans are made (v. 26—before they receive a "spirit")

The same verb *asah* is also used to describe the way that plants "make" fruit (vv. 11, 12), the way that God "made" Eve from Adam's rib (2:18), and, later, when Adam and Eve "made" themselves clothes to wear (3:7). In all these cases, something is made from other things that already exist.

The third way that God is described working is by giving permission—he says "let" this thing happen. The implication is that creation is waiting for God's permission to let it continue:

- Let there be light (v. 3) after the creation of all matter. This presumably was the point when the stars ignited, about half a billion years after the big bang.[2]

---

2. See Starts with a Bang, "What Was It Like When the First Stars Began Illuminating the Universe?" (TinyURL.com/FirstStarlight).

- Let the atmosphere form (v. 6). This was the point when some of the water became water vapor.

- Let the land rise out of the sea and be separate (v. 9). In old-earth terminology, this was when plate tectonics produced land masses and mountains.

- Let plants grow (v. 11), with seeds that continue to make new plants.

- Let the sun and moon appear (v. 14). In old-earth interpretations, this was when they first became visible as the atmosphere cleared (v. 14).[3]

- Let animals grow (vv. 20, 24).

This outline implies that God intervenes at a few key points in creation, and that he also "lets" his creation carry on doing what he wants.

One surprising thing is that the start of life is not described as an act of "creating" life out of nothing (*bara*), or "making" life from preexisting things (*asah*). It is one of those permissive statements where God releases his creation to get on with it—he "lets" plants and animals form, just as he "lets" the land rise to form mountains. This may suggest that the start of life is actually part of a natural process built into creation, so there is a chance that scientists will eventually figure out how it happened.

Another interesting point is that God "created" the first animal and first human being (vv. 21, 27). In the outline above, I suggested that these represent the first life on earth that was given a soul and the first life that was given a spirit, respectively.

---

3. See chap. 8, "Six Snapshots of Creation."

(For the distinction between soul and spirit, see chap. 16, "Animals Have Souls in the Bible," and chap. 17, "What Does the Human Spirit Do?"). If this is the reason for using "create" at these points, it explains why the text also says that God "made" humans (v 26). This "made" would refer to the long process in the ancestry of humans before the creative moment when God "breathed" into Adam (Gen 2:7)—that is, when he received a spirit. Immediately after this, God introduced the first human being to the concept of obedience and the tree that tested morality (vv. 8–9). This implies that he was no longer merely a clever animal, but a spiritual being with moral faculties.

This initial period of creation in Genesis 1 wasn't the end of God's hands-on intervention. The Bible tells us that God intervenes at various times by means of miracles and revelations, and that he constantly communicates personally with his people. However, that miracles are recorded rarely in the Bible implies that God rarely intervenes in this way. Most of what happens on earth is due to the natural processes that God has built into his creation. He continues to permit life to grow and develop, and the sun rises each day without needing permission or prompting from God.

THOUSANDS OR BILLIONS OF YEARS?

Can we decide whether this process of creation occurred over billions of years or over the period of a week?

Scientific studies have concluded that the Earth is 4.5 billion years old and that life began some 3.5 billion years ago. Young-earth theorists have made commendable progress in developing different theories to explain the facts, rather than simply rejecting them like some theologians did in Galileo's day. A few, unfortunately, have acted like flat-earthers, simply shutting their eyes to anything that disagrees with their conclusions.

Some young-earth organizations continue to interact in detail with the sciences—especially Creation Research, Answers in Genesis, Creation Ministries International, and the Institute for Creation Research. Some individuals and organizations from the traditional sciences have responded seriously—for example, BioLogos and Eye on the ICR, which often deal with issues in commendable depth, though most others have ignored them.[4] Recently young-earth theories have been getting a lot of new attention from educators in countries such as Indonesia, Pakistan, and Turkey who are searching for ways to teach a form of biology that agrees with the Qur'an.[5]

Personally I find the young-earth arguments increasingly difficult. A global flood simply can't account for all of geology. The Gunnison River can only cut through the granite of Black Canyon at a maximum rate of one inch a century (much faster than now), and yet it is half a mile deep.[6] The attempt to discredit dating methods is increasingly difficult now that there are so many to verify each other: carbon-14, tree rings, ice cores, growth rings on mollusk shells, beryllium-10, and about forty other methods that are all in rough agreement.[7] It is easy for a nonspecialist to assume that all radiometric measurements are simply wrong, but it is harder to dismiss continuous ice cores that record each summer and winter for the last 160,000 years,

---

4. See, e.g., Eye on the ICR, "Nathaniel Jeanson's Null Hypothesis" (TinyURL. com/JeansonNull).

5. See I Love You But You're Going to Hell, "The Surprising History of Turkey's Creationism" (TinyURL.com/TurkeysHistory).

6. See Wikipedia, "Black Canyon of the Gunnison National Park" (TinyURL. com/GunnisonCanyon).

7. See Dr. Roger C. Wiens, "Radiometric Dating: A Christian Perspective" (TinyURL.com/WiensDating).

which agree with tree rings whose overlapping patterns have recorded the warmth of every summer for 11,500 years.[8]

GENETIC FAMILY TREES

The explosion of information in genetics should now decide the debate. Complete human genomes of people from all over the planet now reveal the family history of the human race. We can follow the inheritance and movements of populations throughout history and verify them by other historical sources.[9] These genetic differences don't usually represent any improvement—they are like the patterns of people's faces by which you can often recognize who is related to whom.

We also have the complete genome of thousands of other species, and we can see that they display the same kinds of tiny differences. These differences also follow family trees, which match the relationships that were predicted by evolutionary theory.[10] These differences can't be related to function, because marsupial squirrels (one of those pouched mammals that developed in isolation in Australia) are genetically distinct from other squirrels even though they look and act almost identically.[11]

The most detailed cross-species work has been done with mitochondrial DNA. Mitochondria are organelles that are present in the cells of every living plant and animal. Their DNA is similar throughout all these species—which is what we would

---

8. Some young-earth theorists are still debating this robustly. See Answers in Genesis, "Do Varves, Tree-Rings, and Radiocarbon Measurements Prove an Old Earth?" (TinyURL.com/Varves).

9. See Wikipedia, "Human Mitochondrial DNA Haplogroup" (TinyURL.com/HumanMitoDNA).

10. See Promega/CURML Workshop Lausanne, "The Use of mtDNA Analysis to Identify Animal Species," November 24, 2015 (TinyURL.com/FumagalliMtDNA).

11. See George B. Johnson, "Convergent and Divergent Evolution," Biology Writer (TinyURL.com/MarsupialSquirrels).

expect, because they always have the same function: to produce energy. Geneticists have long known that there are small variations in the mitochondrial DNA of different species, and much smaller variations within each species. They were first studied in humans, and then in the drosophila fly, and now these genes have been mapped in about six thousand species.[12]

When this inheritance in each species is constructed into a tree pattern, it matches the pattern that describes the differences in anatomy—that is, both genetics and anatomy imply the same evolutionary relationships. This might be expected if these genetic differences had an effect on, for example, the rate at which energy was converted—so that faster animals were able to produce a burst of energy. However, these differences occur mostly in areas that have no effect on the function of mitochondria. They confer no advantage to the animals that have them and are presumably caused by occasional accidents in duplication or individual mutations. Inheriting this kind of change doesn't aid or hinder the next generation—but it does help us to trace their ancestry.

DNA includes more than just the genes that mirror the shape and function of an animal. For example, human DNA includes about ninety-eight thousand fragments of DNA originating from viruses. These were embedded during infections in one of our ancestors before the immune system defeated it, and a harmless fragment of DNA from that virus was passed on to their children. Most of these infections occurred a very long time ago, to

---

12. See Dennis V. Lavrov and Walker Pett, "Animal Mitochondrial DNA as We Do Not Know It," *Genome Biology and Evolution* 8, no. 9 (September 2016): 2896–2913 (TinyURL.com/AnimalMitoDNA).

ancestors who were apes or even worms. The same fragments of virus DNA can be traced through this very long ancestral tree.[13]

To explain these fragments of ancient viruses without involving evolution, we would have to theorize that God deliberately inserted these bits of virus DNA into Adam. In fact, we only have those bits of DNA that we would have if we had descended in the way implied by our biology. That is, fragments that are found in all mammals or in all vertebrates are also found in humans, but fragments found only in birds or only in insects are not found in humans. These pieces of DNA generally make no difference to us—they are harmless accidents of history. But if God did deliberately insert these exact fragments into Adam's DNA, they presumably *would* have a purpose. Was the purpose to make Adam *appear* to be related to all the other animals so that he *seemed* to have an evolutionary past?

God could have deliberately placed these family-tree patterns into our DNA, along with an apparent age for everything else in his creation. However, I can't imagine any purpose except to make us believe in evolution—when eventually we developed the technology to see these patterns. A simpler explanation is that all life is related, and that God created us over a very long period of time, as the evidence found in nature implies.

13. See Carl Zimmer, "Ancient Viruses Are Buried in Your DNA," *New York Times*, October 4, 2017 (TinyURL.com/AncientViruses), and Wikipedia, "Endogenous Retrovirus" (TinyURL.com/WikiRetrovirus).

SUMMARY

- The text in Genesis 1 can be interpreted in several ways.

- God is described as creating from nothing, making things from other things, and allowing natural processes of development.

- There are now so many dating techniques that verify each other that it is unreasonable to doubt them all.

- Genetic relationships mirror those predicted by evolution, even in DNA that is unrelated to shape or function.

- *Proposal:* A great deal of evidence suggests that all life is related through a family tree spanning billions of years. These relationships were not created by God merely to make the world appear to be old.

11

▼

How Big Was the Flood?

Did the waters cover the all the "mountains" of the "earth" or all the "hills" of the "land"? Interpreting the text very literally resolves these ambiguities and produces a surprising conclusion.

Cambridge, where I live, is very flat. People joke that Hills Road is named after its humpback railway bridge. Most of the surrounding countryside is reclaimed marshes, so I can easily imagine a flood covering everything as far as the eye can see. But the idea of Noah's flood covering the whole Earth and all its mountains is much more difficult to envisage. How could millions of land species be rescued in one boat? How did river and sea life survive in mixed salt and fresh water? How did land plants survive underwater for a year? It wasn't just seeds that survived, because the dove found a full-grown olive tree. And the Bible text itself implies some awkward questions concerning this interpretation.

Various organizations have made valiant efforts to explain all the problems using scientific language, though many would dispute that these groups are really employing scientific methods. The methodology of science is to follow the facts to a conclusion, but there is a temptation in this kind of situation to find the facts that fit a predetermined conclusion. There has been a robust debate concerning the science of a worldwide flood,[1] but in this chapter I will concentrate on what the text itself says.

It would be easy to interpret the text in some kind of myth-ological way or to conclude that it is merely an exaggerated account of a small flood. This may, of course, be correct, but I want to take a serious look at the actual text to see what it says as a plain narrative. One problem is that we are too familiar with it—we all know the story of a worldwide flood and God's rescue mission for every land species on the planet. In light of this, it is easy to overlook details in the Bible text itself that imply something else.

HEBREW AMBIGUITIES

The text of the story in the Bible is not straightforward, because the Hebrew text has some important ambiguities:

- Genesis 8:9 says the flood was "over all the surface of the earth." The word "earth" (*erets*) is used in the Bible to mean

  1. the planet "Earth" (e.g., Gen 1:1), *or*

  2. a "land," as in the phrase "the land of Israel" (e.g., twice in Ezek 20:38).

- Genesis 7:20 says that the water rose twenty-three feet above the highest *har*. This word is used in the

---

1. See defenses of the global flood position at Answers in Genesis, "Noah's Ark" (TinyURL.com/ArkForReal), and John Matthews, "Chalk and 'Upper Cre-taceous' Deposits Are Part of the Noachian Flood," March 25, 2009 (TinyURL.com/ChalkDeposits). And see the practical problems with this listed by Mark Isaak, "Problems with a Global Flood," *The Talk Origins Archive* (TinyURL.com/IsaakFlood). Also see chap. 9, "Everyone Believes in Evolution."

Bible for anything from a "mountain" (e.g., twice in Exod 19:18) to a "hill" (e.g., three times in 1 Kgs 16:24). And it is even used for the small hillock on which David stood to speak so that he could be heard by his men standing at the bottom (1 Sam 26:13). So this could mean either

1. the highest mountain on the planet, *or*

2. the highest hill in the land.

- Genesis 7:19 says the waters covered the area "under the entire heavens" (*tachat kol hasha-mayim*). This phrase can mean "everywhere" without limits (e.g., Deut 4:19) or from horizon to horizon (e.g., Job 37:3). It is used, for example, to refer to the lands bordering Palestine that had heard about Israel's invasion (Deut 2:25). As they certainly didn't hear about Israel's conquests in America, in this instance it must mean "from horizon to horizon." So the phrase can mean either

1. all the area under the sky of the whole planet, *or*

2. everywhere under the visible sky at least as far as the horizon.

Therefore, the text could describe a flood that covered every "mountain" of the "planet Earth" or one that covered every "hill" in a large "land" at least as far as the horizon. Either way, the flood was clearly awesome and devastating—it covered the equivalent of a three-story house on the highest hills as far as the eye could see. Noah could see no land even from the top of his boat, which was forty-five feet high. At that height, the horizon is only nine miles away, though the Ararat mountains are tall enough to be seen around the Earth's curvature from a distance of 165 miles.[2] In both cases, the grandeur of the language implies it was a huge flood that completely destroyed that ancient civilization.

ARCHAEOLOGY

Archaeologists in the 1930s found evidence of an amazingly widespread flood (or floods) before 3000 BC, which covered large areas of the Tigris and Euphrates rivers—the Mesopotamian plain covering 140,000 square miles. This wasn't just a shallow flood; even the silt they found deposited by this water was six feet deep.[3] The whole country is flat, with just a few small hills, so this flood would have been utterly devastating; there is simply no high ground to run to for hundreds of miles. This area was the homeland of the ancient Middle Eastern world, and the whole population living there must have been wiped out by this flood. A disaster of this proportion—wiping out a whole civilization—has never been seen anywhere since in the world.

According to the account in Genesis 8, the rain was followed by a strong wind (v. 1), which apparently blew the ark toward the Ararat mountains, where it "came to rest on [or among] the mountains" (v. 4). Then there was a wait of three months before "the tops of the mountains became visible" (v. 5). The Hebrew text does not actually specify whether the ark rested "on" or "among" the mountains for these three months. The word

---

2. See Wikipedia, "Horizon" (TinyURL.com/HowFarHorizon).
3. See "Tigris and Euphrates Floods," Global Security (TinyURL.com/IraqDeluge).

"rest" (Hebrew *nuach*) has two meanings—"to stop" or "to have peace"—though usually it implies both, that is, no longer having to move or struggle. For example, God gave Israel "rest" in the land of Canaan (Deut 12:10; 25:19; Josh 1:13, 15, etc.), but that didn't mean they couldn't move about in the land. This means there are two possible scenarios:

1. the ark could "rest on" the top of the highest peak— that is, be grounded there until the other peak appeared three months later, *or*

2. the ark could "rest among" the mountains—that is, having been becalmed when the strong wind stopped, it gradually drifted for three months until both mountain peaks were in view.

THE RAVEN AND DOVE

The deciding factor between these two options is found in the account of the birds that were released forty days after the peaks of the mountains became visible. Genesis says that the first was a raven, who "kept flying back and forth until the water had dried up from the earth" (Gen 8:7). Presumably, being a carrion bird, it could land and feed on floating corpses even if it found no land. By contrast, the second was a dove, who "could find nowhere to perch because there was water over all the surface of the earth; so it returned to Noah in the ark" (v. 9). After a week, he sent the dove out again, and when it "returned to him in the evening, there in its beak was a freshly plucked olive leaf" (v. 11). This can help us decide between the two possible scenarios.

The mountains of Ararat consist of two peaks: Greater Ararat, 5,140 meters high, and Little Ararat, 3,925 meters high.[4] If the ark had come to rest "on" the highest, Noah would have seen no other peaks until the water receded another 1,200 meters, so this might explain why he had to wait three months before seeing the top of any mountain. However, by the time that lower peak was visible, the water would have sunk to the 3,900-meter contour line on Greater Ararat, the mountain that they were resting on, so they would have been surrounded by twenty-five square miles of dry land. After another forty days, when the first bird was released, this area would have grown considerably because the mountain has a plateau at about 3,000 meters. In this situation, it is difficult to understand why the text says the birds couldn't find any land. Indeed, they would have had to fly many miles before they found any water.

Therefore, the text must mean that the ark "came to rest among the mountains." That is, the ark came to a peaceful calm in the vicinity of Ararat, from where Noah could see the mountain peaks start to appear. This would also explain why the text mentions the plural "tops" of the mountains (v. 5) — if the ark had been sitting on top of one of them, Noah wouldn't have seen them both. It also explains why it says that the ark came to rest at "the mountains of Ararat" (v. 4) — the plural suggests the area rather than a single mountaintop.

This meaning of "rest" introduces yet another pair of possible interpretations, because the text does not make clear where the peaks were spotted.

It says the "tops of the mountains became visible" (v. 5). This could mean either that:

---

4. See Wikipedia, "Mount Ararat" (TinyURL.com/WikiArarat) and "Little Ararat" (TinyURL.com/WikiLittleArarat).

1. the ark was becalmed within the mountain range itself and the peaks gradually became visible as the water level dropped, *or*

2. that it was becalmed some way off and the mountains became visible as the ark slowly drifted closer.

The account of the birds can help us determine between these two options as well. The mountain range is not large—the two peaks are only about seven miles apart—so if the ark became becalmed within the mountain range, it would have been a short distance to the visible peaks. The birds could have seen the peaks clearly and reached them easily, so neither of them would have returned. Therefore, the ark must have been becalmed some distance from the actual mountains.

If the ark stopped some way distant from the Ararat mountains, this helps to explain some other details in the text. First, the dove managed to reach land the second time, though it couldn't reach it during the previous week, even though the peaks had already been visible before the first flight (vv. 5, 8). This makes sense if the ark was floating toward those peaks. Second, the text says, "There was water over all the surface of the earth," even though the peaks had already been visible for over a month (v. 9). This language makes sense if the mountain peaks were a long way off over the horizon (i.e., more than nine miles away), so it was still true that the ark was surrounded by water from horizon to horizon.

Examining the text has narrowed down the possibilities. We can conclude that the ark was blown toward the Ararat mountains and was becalmed some distance from them—but how far? People who train homing pigeons (which is the same species as a dove) say that they can cover fifty or a hundred miles without training, though this can be increased to five hundred miles with training.[5] So if the ark was drifting toward the visible peaks, and it was too far away for the dove but close enough a week later for the same dove, we could conclude that it was something like fifty miles away when the dove reached it. This means the mountain peaks were visible far beyond the horizon (which is only nine miles distant), so the phrase "there was water over all the surface of the earth" (v. 9) could still apply.

GLOBAL OR LOCAL?

This brings us to the crucial question: did the flood cover the whole of the *planet* or the whole of the *land*?

Surprisingly we haven't found any details in the text that conflict with the idea that the flood covered the 144,000 square miles of the Tigris-Euphrates basin rather than covering the planet. This low-lying area has only shallow hills and is surrounded by higher land that encloses the plain, which certainly *can* flood. And there is archaeological evidence that this area *did* experience a catastrophic flood within a time period consistent with Genesis.

It is understandable that the worldwide flood interpretation is popular because the text has two phrases that appear to imply this: "under the entire heavens" (Gen 7:19) and "over all the surface of the earth" (8:9). However, as we saw above, the former can be used with the sense of from horizon to horizon (Job 37:3; Deut 2:25), and the second occurs *after* the mountain peaks have become visible beyond the horizon (Gen 8:5, 9)—so this phrase must mean something like "as far as the horizon." We might complain that this isn't the way that we understand these phrases in English, but the important issue is what these phrases

---

5. See Wikipedia, "Homing Pigeon" (TinyURL.com/WikiPigeons).

mean in the Bible text—otherwise we may end up imposing our own meanings on the Bible.

In the New Testament, the word *kosmos* is used to describe the "world" that Noah's flood destroyed (Heb 11:7; 2 Pet 2:5). This word is often used in the New Testament for the evil systems of a corrupt society (John 15:19; 17:16; 1 Cor 2:12; Gal 6:14; Jas 1:27; 4:4; 2 Pet 1:4; 1 John 5:4). That meaning explains why Hebrews says that Noah "condemned the world." Clearly the planet of animals, plants, and rocks weren't morally evil, so the word "condemned" couldn't refer to them. However, the civilization that Noah lived among *was* condemned as evil, and the Greek *kosmos* often refers to a corrupt system. This suggests that the "world" that was drowned in Noah's day refers to the evil civilization he lived among, and not the planet they lived on.

The details about Noah in the Bible text are therefore compatible with the interpretation that this flood covered all the hills in the land that Noah and his civilization lived in, leaving his family as the only survivors, floating in a boat on water that stretched as far as the eye could see. What about the other interpretation—that the waters covered the whole planet?

The Bible text presents a serious problem with the idea that the whole planet was flooded: the olive leaf brought by the dove. In the timetable of the text, the peaks of the mountains appeared only seven weeks before the leaf was found (Gen 8:5–11). This means there was a very short period for a tree that had been drowned for seven months to rejuvenate and sprout new leaves. Actually, the time available is much less, because olive trees don't grow above 1,000 meters,[6] and the highest peak of the Ararat mountains is 5,140 meters, and the next is about 4,000 meters.

---

6. See Mariela Torres et al., "Olive Cultivation in the Southern Hemisphere," *Frontiers in Plant Science* 8 (October 2017) (TinyURL.com/OlivesWater).

Therefore, the water had to drop 3.000 meters (over two miles) after "the tops of the mountains became visible" (v. 5) before the olive trees would have been uncovered.

The Jewish rabbis, who took the Bible text very seriously, found a way to interpret the text so that the flood could cover the whole world *and* leave a healthy olive tree to provide this leaf. They reasoned that the Lord loved the land of Israel, so he would protect it from flooding.[7] Therefore the dove must have flown to the Mount of Olives and returned with a fresh leaf—a round trip of about two thousand miles. Protecting Israel from floodwaters would, of course, require a wall as tall as Everest around the whole country, but once this is granted, it is possible to reconcile the Bible text with the idea of a worldwide flood.

LITERAL MEANING

Therefore, while it is possible to conclude that the Bible text refers to a flood covering the whole planet, the text actually implies a flood that covered the land in which Noah was living. Reading the text as actually found in the Bible suggests that waters covered all the "hills" in the "land." The civilization of Noah's day occupied the huge, low-lying Tigris-Euphrates plain. The text implies that the ark was blown by "a strong wind" until the two "mountain tops" of Ararat became visible. When the dove was released, it reached the higher land that had not been flooded, where living trees were still growing. When the floodwaters retreated, Noah was able to let out the animals and restart farming.

The ark was needed to save not only Noah and his family but also the animals. They represented the most valuable products of

---

7. See Genesis Rabbah 33:5–6 at Visual Midrash, "Noah and the Flood" (TinyURL.com/NoahMidrash8).

that civilization, which had grown large and prosperous because the people had learned to farm crops and livestock. It took many generations to breed docile cattle from huge and dangerous wild bovines such as aurochs. We take farm animals for granted, but none of them were found in the wild—they all had to be bred by early farmers. The land also needed other animals and birds to provide a fully functioning ecology. Some of these wild species might have recolonized from surrounding areas, but the natural barriers of desert and mountains would have made this a slow process, so Noah was told to take some of these species too. But he only needed the local species—not everything in the whole world. And he didn't need to take fish, which would come back into the area via the rivers when the flood ended.

This is the story we find by a literal reading of the Genesis narrative. It describes an extraordinary event: Noah would have needed miraculous help from God to know that he should build an ark, and perhaps to get the wild animals into the ark. But the account in the Bible text itself doesn't tell us that the water covered the whole planet, so there is no major conflict with what we have learned from science.

SUMMARY

- The Hebrew is ambiguous about whether the flood covered every "mountain"/"hill" in the "earth"/"land" from "under all heaven"/"horizon to horizon."

- The phrase "there was water over all the surface of the earth/land" was still true forty days after the "tops of the mountains became visible" (Gen 8:5-9).

- Details of the story concerning the birds and the olive leaf do not make sense if the flood was global.

- Archaeology shows evidence of a flood that covered the whole country of Mesopotamia.

- *Proposal:* The flood drowned the civilization occupying the 140,000-square-mile Mesopotamian plain. Noah's ark was blown toward the Ararat mountains.

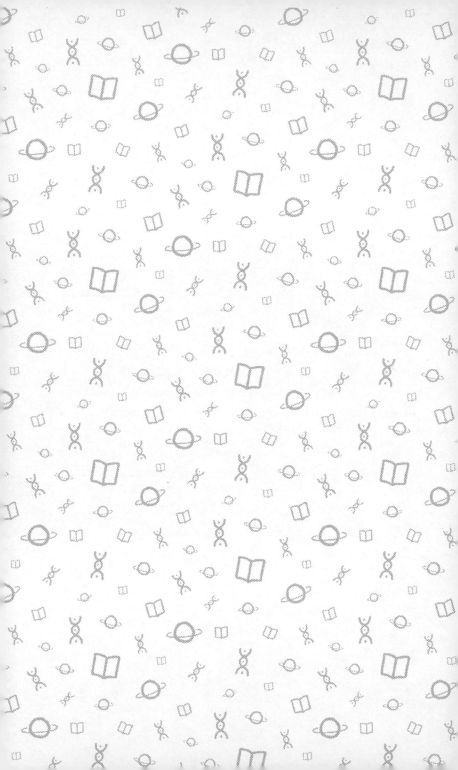

12

▾

Babel Rediscovered

Were languages "created" or "confused" at Babel? The actual tower was rediscovered a few decades ago, thanks to a deciphered Babylonian tablet. Its Sumerian name suggests why it was so dangerous.

The story of the Tower of Babel (Gen 11) sounds like an ancient folktale to explain the origin of languages. At first glance, it seems to say that everyone in the world lived in one country until God gave them different languages in order to scatter them. We now know that this is not what happened, because historical comparisons of languages show they have gradually grown from each other—a growth that we can still see occurring.[1] Does this mean that we have to dismiss the story in Genesis as a simplistic myth? A close look at the Bible text tells us a different story—one that doesn't contradict philology and comparative linguistics.

It is joked that the last word spoken at Babel was "sack" because this sound means the same thing—a type of bag—in a very wide variety of languages (e.g., French *sac*, Greek *sakoon*, Latin *saccus*, Spanish *saco*, Filipino *sako*, Hebrew *saq*, Afrikaans *sak*, and Russian *meshok*). Of course, there are many other such

---

1. For an overview, see Wikipedia, "Indo-European Languages" (TinyURL. com/LanguageSpread).

examples of word similarities across languages, and they exist because languages are related to one another. Many European languages developed from Latin, while also imbibing words from other languages such as Norse. In the same way, ancient Hebrew is related to Akkadian and Ugarit, with loanwords inherited from places such as Egypt. These Semitic languages later developed into Syriac, Arabic, and Swahili.

Complex family trees have been drawn to trace the history of all languages, and these successfully explain the origins of language diversity. Every time a population splits by moving apart, its accents and vocabulary diverge until they form separate dialects; and when their languages become sufficiently different, the people become "foreigners" to each other. So why does this Bible story say that the first ancient languages split by means of a miracle? Did the people at Babel really walk away speaking ancient versions of Egyptian, Hebrew, Ugaritic, Akkadian, Hittite, and Greek? Since then, other languages such as Swahili and Lingala have grown up as new languages relatively recently. The most widely spoken language in the world is English, which now has a vocabulary of about a million words, but this did not start developing until the Middle Ages. If new languages are still developing, why should the ancient languages need a miraculous origin? In fact, the Bible doesn't say this at all.

LANGUAGES BEFORE BABEL

The chapter *before* the Babel incident says that "maritime peoples spread out into their territories by their clans within their nations, each with its own language" (Gen 10:5, with examples in vv. 20, 31). This tells us what we already know—that when people move a long distance or overseas, they develop their own individual language. Every generation of teenagers invents new words or new meanings of old words, and if there is no wider society to communicate with, this becomes the new way of speaking. Therefore, Genesis 10 tells us that the nations were united initially by family ties, but each nation formed its own language when it traveled to its own land. This is the same process that philologists have shown happening in the world today.

The next chapter in Genesis tells the story of Babel. This is a completely different type of event—a nation that was united around a common goal and forcibly split up so that it wouldn't succeed. The text doesn't say that any new languages were created at Babel. It says that the Lord *confused the language* (11:7, 9). This means the people there shared one language, but suddenly they couldn't understand each other anymore—as if they had lost their ability to speak properly or to understand properly.

There is no indication that they spoke a single worldwide language, or that this confusion was a worldwide phenomenon, because the phrase translated "the whole world" (in Gen 11:1) can also mean "the whole land." The Hebrew word *erets* can mean "land," as in "land (*erets*) of Israel."[2] The phrase translated "the whole earth" in Genesis 11:1 (*khol ha'arets*) occurs also in Genesis 13:9, where Abraham showed Lot "the whole land" of Canaan and invited him to choose where he wanted to live.

In any case, Genesis 10 has already recorded that various family clans had moved to a different "land" (*erets*), and this chapter says some people went to the "land [*erets*] of Shinar" (Gen 11:2). So, when the adjacent verse says "the whole *erets* had one language," we can assume this *erets* means "land," just as it does in the previous and following verses.

This happened in Shinar, the name for what later became Babylon (Gen 11:2; Dan 1:2). This is the site of the earliest city civilization, where society was first organized into specialties:

---

2. As we saw in chap. 11, "How Big Was the Flood?"

farming, building, accounting, religion, and fighting. As in many other population centers, the rulers consolidated their hold over the people by uniting them in a huge building project, for example Stonehenge and Mayan temples. This tower was a visible sign that held the people together and reminded them that their strength came from working together for a common purpose. We don't know what the purpose was in this case, but Genesis suggests that if they had continued, they would have become unstoppable. God said: "If as one people speaking the same language they have begun to do this, then nothing they plan to do will be impossible for them" (Gen 11:6). He stopped them by making everyone unintelligible to their neighbors.

ZIGGURAT

This story of this tower wasn't regarded as a myth in the ancient world because the tower wasn't lost until about 300 BC. It had not been finished, because it was abandoned when the people couldn't understand each other, but everyone in the ancient world knew of it and could travel to see it. Modern scholars have often thought it was the great ziggurat at Babylon, and new evidence has shown this was essentially correct. Recent scholarship has confirmed that this wasn't the actual tower of Babel, but it was built on top of a very ancient structure that can be traced back to at least 1700 BC and is likely to be much older. Although pyramid-shaped towers called ziggurats were found throughout Mesopotamia, this one was different: it was larger than normal, and it is now known that the original builders didn't finish it.

An inscription found several decades ago that has recently been studied has given us the forgotten history of this monument. It is a record left by Nebuchadnezzar II, who eventually did finish building the tower, in the sixth century BC, at least a thousand years (and probably much longer) after it had been abandoned. His inscription records: "A former king built it ... but he did not complete its head. Since a remote time, people had abandoned it."[3] The unfinished original had no top layer, so rain had entered and disintegrated the mud bricks from the inside. This meant Nebuchadnezzar had to virtually rebuild it before he could add his own temple at the top. When finished, it was ninety meters high with more than thirty million hand-made bricks, making it the greatest wonder of the ancient world. Imagine something as tall as a thirty-story building in a flat land that has no hills for hundreds of miles. It must have been more awesome than the NASA rocket hangars in the flatlands of Cape Canaveral.

Unfortunately, Alexander the Great ordered the tower to be demolished so that he could rebuild a better one, but he died before he could start the project. All that remains is the foundation, which excavations have found to extend a long way underground. It is clear from what is left that the size was not exaggerated. The inscription that was discovered included an engraving that reveals the shape of Nebuchadnezzar's rebuilt version: a stepped ziggurat with a very tall first stage and an extraordinary large temple at the top.

AN INDIANA JONES STORY

The inscription was originally found at Babylon in 1917 by three archaeologists. They recognized that this was Nebuchadnezzar's message of dedication for the tower and realized how important it was. It was carved on a stele (a large stone tablet) that had been broken into three pieces. Events then unfolded like an Indiana Jones story. Realizing that the worsening world war was bringing armies to the area, the archaeologists decided to

---

3. See Wikipedia, "Tower of Babel" (TinyURL.com/WikiBabel).

ensure the safety of the stele by removing it from the country. They each took a piece to their homes—to Germany, London, and the US. The first two pieces are now on view in the Schoyen Collection.[4] But the third one—which includes a floor plan of the temple built on the top—has disappeared somewhere in the US.[5] I imagine that someone will one day turn these events into a movie, where they'll find the missing piece and discover the floor plan includes a treasure map!

Ancient people like Nebuchadnezzar must have wondered why this tower had never been completed, and the Bible gave them the answer: God interrupted the building project. But what was so wrong about building a tower whose top would reach to the heavens (Gen 11:4)? Was God the first NIMBY? Or did he perhaps want to stop the people's study of astrology, their idolatry, or their self-satisfied pride? Maybe, like the Aztec pyramids, the structure was being built to perform human sacrifices at the summit. We really have no idea because no records have survived from so long ago to tell us.

One clue lies in its Sumerian name: E-temen-anki, which in ancient Sumerian meant "House of the Foundation of Heaven and Earth," as if this formed a physical gateway to the gods.[6] This can't be a name that the Babylonians invented, because their language was Akkadian, and this name is in the much more ancient language of Sumerian, which was spoken in the third millennium BC. The last native speaker of Sumerian died more than a thousand years before Nebuchadnezzar decided to rebuild this

4. See Schoyen Collection, "Tower of Babel Stele" (TinyURL.com/BabelStele).

5. See a scholarly article by A. R. George, "The Tower of Babel: Archaeology, History and Cuneiform Texts," *Archiv für Orientforschung* 51 (2005–2006): 75–95 (TinyURL.com/GeorgeBabel).

6. See Wikipedia, "Etemenanki" (TinyURL.com/WikiEtemenanki), and Jona Lendering, "Etemenanki (the 'Tower of Babel')," Livius (TinyURL.com/BabelRuins).

strangely named monument. The name sounds very similar to how Genesis describes it: "a tower that reaches to the heavens." This Bible phrase sounds innocent—as if it merely describes something very tall—but the full version in Sumerian implies that they wanted to communicate with both heaven above and the underworld beneath. Perhaps this physical object represented some dangerous spiritual experimentation.

The Bible itself says that the danger lay in the people's unity, because God warned that if humans all worked together there was nothing they couldn't do (Gen 11:4-6). After all, when humans get organized, they can become very dangerous. They do things like building enough bombs to destroy the planet, wiping out large numbers of species, or burning enough fossil fuel to change the climate.[7]

One modern equivalent of the Tower of Babel is the way that humanity is now interconnected via the internet. This is a fantastic achievement, but it does give us a glimpse of the danger that God predicted. A few angry extremists in disparate countries can now get together to organize terrorist attacks that kill thousands and disrupt the lives of millions of people. Sexual predators, bullies, and identity thieves can find victims anywhere in the world. The internet can spread hatred, misinformation, and also all kinds of dangerous information. As an experiment I researched how to make a radioactive bomb from easily sourced components. The search didn't take long—but I hope the secret services didn't follow my research trail.

This "reverse Babel effect" is also producing wonderfully good and helpful benefits. Every area of research, from medicine to biblical studies, progresses much faster by sharing information. Specialists who previously met only at conferences can

---

7. See chap. 14, "Ecology and the New Earth."

now be in constant communication. We feared that computers would isolate people, but translation tools and social networking are bringing people together in ways previously impossible. Many of us now have more "friends" than we have time for. Governments are finding it harder to secretly oppress their populations because they can't block phone videos from telling the truth about what is happening in the world. One consequence is that governments find it increasingly difficult to convince their people that another country deserves to be attacked. Another consequence is that everyone—even foolish or evil people—can just as easily spread lies and hatred.

Will the internet ultimately bring good or evil? We have survived many potential world-breaking crises: two world wars, a Cold War with missiles on a hair trigger, a population explosion saved by an agricultural revolution, and a rescued ozone layer. We have survived these by working together, and the internet is helping us to cooperate more and more. But Revelation may have a disturbing comment about a danger that will come from the internet: translate "666" into Hebrew numbers and you get "www"! Perhaps this is laughably pessimistic, but could it be ultimately realistic? Will online banking, trading, and working eventually produce a society where each life can be controlled by the state?

The world *will* need to be rescued from the brink at least one more time by Jesus' return, but in the meantime, the church is here to restrain evil and delay the coming of that day (2 Thess 2:6). In the world of the internet, every user counts, and everyone can contribute. Each individual user can powerfully affect many others, for both good and evil. Fake news that stirs up hatred can be combated with facts, and conflicts based on religious or ethnic tribalism can be dissipated by talking to each other.

We can all ensure that this new ease of communication doesn't unite us into disparate communities that each want to take over the world. Instead of building a tower to highlight the importance of our own group, we should be integrating and befriending people in groups where we don't naturally belong. We can work to bring everyone into a unity under God—not a unity against everyone else who doesn't live in our land. That plan didn't work out so well last time.

SUMMARY

- New languages develop when populations become isolated.

- This had already happened before Babel (Gen 10:5, 20, 31).

- The language of the "world"/"land" of Shinar was "confused" to make the people scatter (Gen 11:1-2, 7-9).

- Nebuchadnezzar built the great ziggurat on the foundation of an ancient tower that was unfinished and abandoned at least a millennium before.

- *Proposal:* The tower united the people around a purpose that God needed to frustrate, so he made them scatter.

13

▾

Joshua's Long Day

The lengthened day was accompanied by another miracle: hailstones that killed the enemy. Meteorologists know a phenomenon that links these two events and helps us to understand how one miracle gave rise to both of these wonders.

One of the strangest passages in the Bible is the extraordinary account, in Joshua 10, of when God made the sun stand still to extend the length of one day. Joshua prayed for this when the Israelite army was defending the Gibeonites, their allies, whose city was under attack. The text tells us that the sun stayed still for a full day—effectively making one day last for forty-eight hours. Skeptics point out that this kind of miracle introduces too many problems to be believable.

For the ancients, this event was unusual, though it was easy enough to explain: God simply stopped the sun moving. Today we understand some of the mechanisms involved: either the earth had to stop spinning or the sun had to start moving. Of course, if God created the universe, and if we accept that he performs miracles, then he could implement either of these options. But the problem with both is that they would pull apart the creation he so lovingly made.

While standing still on the earth's surface, we are actually spinning at one thousand miles per hour; if the spin were to decelerate at the rate of a car doing an emergency stop, it would take seventeen minutes for the planet to come to a halt. If you were on a car's roof during an emergency stop you'd fly off and land in the road. Likewise, people on the surface of a decelerating earth would fly through the air while buildings and trees collapsed. Even if the deceleration were much slower, it would destabilize earthquake zones, and the moon would drive unimaginable tsunamis around the globe. If, instead, the sun started moving around the earth, it would need to reach a speed of twenty-five million miles an hour to "stand still" in the sky. To reach that speed—even if it accelerated at the same planet-tearing rate we've considered—would take nineteen days.

MISSING-DAY MYTH

Stories of NASA finding a "missing day" are easy to find on the internet. The most common one says that an engineer visiting NASA overheard some astronomers who were confused by the fact that when they wound back the star maps, there appeared to be a whole day missing from the calculations. The problem with this story is that there is no kind of data that could ever discover a missing day. When astronomical calculations "wind back the star clock" they are based on present-day movements, so any missing day would be invisible because we have nothing to check our dates against. Exact dates in ancient Chinese and Babylonian records are themselves determined by these astronomical calculations, so they can't be used to confirm them. The man behind NASA's urban myth has now been traced—he was a heating engineer sent to look at the boiler—but the missing day itself remains ... missing.[1]

---

1. See "NASA Discovers a 'Lost Day' in Time?," Snopes (TinyURL.com/MissingDay).

Nevertheless, a literal interpretation of Joshua 10 is still possible without the earth or sun actually changing its movement. To investigate what happened, we have to put aside our preconceived interpretations and take seriously the facts that are present in the text itself.

The first question is whether the sun itself stopped moving relative to the earth or whether people stopped seeing any movement. Of course, we already know that the sun itself didn't stop moving, because it wasn't moving in the first place. This isn't really an issue, because we still refer to relative movements—even a modern astronomer might say, "I'll meet you at sunrise," without implying the sun literally rises in the sky. We can conclude from this phrase that the Israelites' *perception* of the sun was that it had stopped moving—that is, its light was continuing to come from the same place—but can we conclude that the sun itself had stopped its relative movement? The question we need to answer is how everyone perceived the sun to have stopped.

This perception can't be dismissed as a matter of their imagination or wishful thinking, because it had incredibly practical consequences. The Israelite army had traveled a long way to come and help their allies. The Gibeonites were being attacked by armies from surrounding cities for siding with the Israelites. The Israelites were winning the battle and their enemies were on the run when the light started failing. If the sun had set, their enemies could have gotten away and hidden in the dark countryside. Then, when the Israelites had gone home (as they'd have to eventually), the opposing armies would have come back to finish the job. So, for their allies to have any hope of sleeping safely, the Israelites had to catch up with these men before they melted away in the encroaching darkness. Joshua, in desperation, prayed a seemingly impossible prayer—that the daylight would be extended until they had caught up with the fleeing enemy (see Josh 10:10–14).

DEADLY HAILSTONES

The second question concerns the role of the extraordinary weather conditions that are recorded in the text: a storm with huge hailstones that killed most of the enemy soldiers (Josh 10:11). Deadly hailstones still occur today. The golf-ball-sized hail that occasionally occurs in the US *can* be fatal. (I won't forget having to hide under a bridge once to escape such hail.) However, much larger hailstones have fallen occasionally. In Bangladesh, hailstones the size of grapefruit killed 92 people in 1986, and 246 people died in India in 1888; as recently as 2009 there were 14 fatalities during a storm in China.[2] Hailstones grow in tall cumulonimbus clouds, which can be miles high. Taller clouds produce larger hailstones, so these clouds must have been exceptionally tall to produce hailstones large enough to kill people.[3]

Can we work out what actually happened when Joshua asked God to keep the sun in the sky? We can only theorize. But before I do that, let me tell you about the evening my family and I set up camp beside Lake Isabella in California. When we arrived, we should have known something was wrong—the parking lot and lakeside were empty. At first, it seemed as though evening was falling early, because the sun descended behind abnormally tall clouds over the western hillsides. These clouds created an amazing sunset that lasted for several hours. Even after the sun had long disappeared behind the hills, the tops of the clouds

---

2. See Dylan Thuras, "Hail No: An Account of the World's Biggest, Deadliest Hailstorms," Atlas Obscura, September 26, 2010 (TinyURL.com/DeadlyHail).

3. See Wikipedia, "Hail" (TinyURL.com/WikiHail).

reflected its light down to us in a hundred shades of red. The sun had already disappeared over the horizon, so it was technically nighttime, and yet it still seemed like early evening. The light was being transmitted from the tall clouds as if they were a giant prism high enough to see the sun that had disappeared around the globe, and also to see us. On hills we could see what was creating this extraordinary cloud: a huge forest fire that was raging uncontrollably across the countryside. It was this fire that had kept all the better-informed visitors away from the area. The blaze was so great that it was creating its own weather system, so in addition to the smoke and soot that it threw up, the heat produced a cloud that was perhaps a mile high in front of the setting sun. It was a disaster that created a beautiful and prolonged afternoon and evening for us.

JOSHUA'S PRAYER

So let's come to my theory. We are told in Joshua 10:12 that when Joshua prayed, the sun was "over Gibeon" (in the west), so it was already starting to descend, and that "the moon stopped" (v. 13), so it was already visible, as it often is on afternoons just before full moon. This prompted him to pray for more time because he thought the day would end before they had caught up with the enemy. The enemy were running from both the Israelites and also the hailstones because, we read, "more of them died from the hail than were killed by the swords of the Israelites" (v. 11).

The Israelites had come to Gibeon from Gilgal in the east, and the enemy ran toward Beth Horon in the west. The tall storm clouds must have been in the west because they were pelting the enemy with hail, though not the Israelites. This means that the sun was disappearing behind these western clouds. It would have made it seem like evening had come early, and Joshua would have started worrying about losing the light.

However, these clouds not only precipitated an early start to the evening—they also prolonged it beyond normal nightfall. Like my family's incredible evening at Lake Isabella, the clouds would continue to deflect the sunlight to light up the land, even after the sun had set below the horizon. The taller the clouds, the longer the sunlight is deflected, and we know the clouds must have been extremely tall to produce such huge hailstones. Normal storm clouds can be a mile high, but clouds that produce such extreme hailstones can be ten miles high.[4]

The evening on that day was therefore longer than anyone had ever experienced, starting much earlier and ending later than normal, due to those extraordinary clouds. But how long was it? Measuring time without a watch and without seeing the position of the sun (which had disappeared behind the cloud) is very difficult, especially on a day filled with exciting events such as a military victory. The sun disappeared from view long before sunset because the extraordinarily tall clouds were to the west—so Joshua's men had no indication of time for much of the day. They knew that it was still daytime, because light was coming through the cloud and they could still see clearly, but it must have seemed like an unending evening that extended even beyond the normal sunset. However tall the cloud was, it could not add an extra day of daylight—but it could have felt like it.

BOOK OF JASHER

Some may complain that if the Bible says there was an extra full day, then the light must have extended by the full twenty-four hours. I'm sympathetic to this kind of thinking, so I regard it significant that the extra day wasn't recorded by a biblical author:

---

4. See Matthew Cappucci, "Supercell: It's the King of Thunderstorms," Science News for Students (TinyURL.com/HailClouds).

it is a quote from a nonbiblical source called the Book of Jasher ("Jashar," NIV). Some interpreters think that the words "as it is written in the book of Jasher" refer to the two verses *before* this phrase rather than the sentence that follows it; however, the exact same phrase occurs at 2 Samuel 1:18, where it clearly refers to the words that follow it. This ancient book—which is now lost—claimed that the sun stopped "in the middle of the heavens for a whole day" (Josh 10:13, my translation). This is difficult to square with the prayer of Joshua, "Sun, stand still over Gibeon" (v. 12). As a midday sun isn't over anything in particular (except oneself), this prayer implies the sun was already significantly descended, so that it could be said to be "over" the city in the west. This contradicts the Book of Jasher, which says it was "in the middle" of the sky.

By the way, the so-called books of Jasher found on various internet sites and sold to the unwary are modern forgeries by Flaccus Albinus in 1751 and J. H. Parry in 1840; even the Hebrew Sepher ha-Jasher ("Book of the Upright") dates back only to the fifteenth century.[5] These have taken the name "Jasher" from the Bible to make their works seem important. The original ancient work is totally lost, unfortunately.

For the original readers, a quote from this ancient source helped to confirm that the extraordinary event had really happened—it was equivalent to citing a credible independent witness. However, quoting an outside source within Scripture does not give it the status of Scripture. If this were so, we would have to agree with the ancient poet who said, "Cretans are always liars, evil brutes, and lazy gluttons" (quoted in Titus 1:12). The inhabitants of Crete might disagree! And we'd have to agree with the person quoted by Paul who said, "It is good for a man not to

---

5. See Wikipedia, "Book of Jasher (Pseudo-Jasher)" (TinyURL.com/PsJasher).

have sexual relations with a woman" (1 Cor 7:1—which Paul disputes in vv. 3–5). So when the Book of Jasher says that daylight was extended by a whole day, this may be an exaggeration or a mistake, but it nevertheless confirms that something amazing happened—daylight lasted much longer that day.

SERIES OF MIRACLES

Does this "natural" explanation mean that God was not involved after all and that there were no miracles that day? The text itself relates an amazing series of miracles. First, a storm produced extraordinarily huge hailstones at exactly the right time and place, so that they fell on the enemy but not on the Israelites. Then these hail clouds—the highest that the Israelites had ever seen—deflected the sunlight to keep it shining on them even after the normal time of sunset and enabled them to continue seeing until they had defeated the enemy. Finally, there was the miracle of Joshua's men, who had marched all night to reach Gibeon (Josh 10:9) and then spent all day fighting and running. Boxers today train for months in order to keep going for ten three-minute rounds; these men were still eager to chase their enemy throughout the lengthened evening after marching all night and fighting all day—a miracle of God-given strength.

It may seem as though the wonder is removed from a Bible story if we try to explain it. However, the facts about the hailstorm that give rise to this interpretation are within the text itself. And it is the text itself that notes the detail that "a whole day" is from an external document rather than being part of the narrator's report. These details in the text allow for two interpretations: they agree with the interpretation that the sun appeared to stop setting for half a day (while hidden behind the storm clouds) and even for some time after sunset, and they also agree with the interpretation that the sun appeared to stop setting for a whole twenty-four hours (while the earth stopped spinning).

When we add facts that we know from scientific studies of nature, we can decide between these different interpretations. First, we can rule out what some interpreters regard as the literal meaning of the text: the sun definitely did not stop moving—because the sun doesn't ever move around the earth. So we have to decide between the two other possible interpretations: that the day was twenty-four hours longer (as the Book of Jasher says) or that it was much longer than expected. We know that human perceptions of time are extremely variable, so without a clock, it is extremely difficult to judge how much time has lapsed. And we know that stopping the earth spinning would have had huge consequences that are not mentioned in Joshua. It is therefore most likely that the extended day was caused by the storm clouds rather than stopping the earth spinning.

SUMMARY

- The sun did not stop (it doesn't move), and stopping the earth has huge consequences.

- The tall hail clouds in the west would make evening appear to come soon and keep deflecting sunlight even after sunset.

- The phrase "a whole day" is quoted from the non-Bible book of Jasher.

- *Proposal:* When the sun disappeared, Joshua prayed for more light, and it extended past sunset, but no one could measure how long.

14

▼

Ecology and the New Earth

Ecologists warn us to look after the world, but the Bible says there will be a "new Earth," so why bother? Details in the Bible text suggest that the Earth will be renewed, not replaced.

Flash Gordon, James Bond, Superman, and Margaret Thatcher. Can't see the connection? Well, when it came to saving planet Earth, the intervention of Mrs. T in the late 1980s was just as dramatic as the exploits of these fictional superheroes. Unlike almost all other political leaders, she had a science background, so she immediately recognized the dire consequences of the growing hole in the ozone layer. She galvanized the world to do something about it, and it is now being dealt with very successfully.[1] What could have been the end of our history is soon to be history itself.

Subsequent politicians have taken much longer to recognize the reality of another threat to the planet: global warming. And now there is a panic, because despite all the available energy from wind and sun, the world is still burning carbon like there's no tomorrow. Much of the coal, oil, and gas that was laid down

---

1. See India Bourke, "Will Margaret Thatcher and Ronald Reagan Be the Unlikely Saviours of the World from Climate Change?," *New Statesman America*, October 14, 2016 (TinyURL.com/ThatcherClimate).

over millions of years has been consumed between the generations of James Watt and Elon Musk. Unexpectedly, the warmer Arctic has extended the polar jet stream to produce alternating extremes of cold and hot, which in turn produce stronger tornados and droughts than before. These unpredicted consequences are on top of the ecological changes and raised sea levels that had been foreseen; and perhaps there will be more surprises around the corner.

Christians have been among the last to take this seriously. Some still regard it as unimportant because of the promise of a "new Earth." The Bible talks about a "renewed," "redeemed," and "restored" Earth, but it never mentions a "replacement" Earth. Isaiah was the first to see a vision of this new Earth, and his vision makes clear that this was still the same structure as the old Earth. He was shown Jerusalem in the new earth, and outside it lay the corpses from the final battle (Isa 66:22–24). The wonderful act of God that Isaiah described was the planet's renewal after a terrible ordeal. It can't have been a replacement planet because God wouldn't have created copies of the corpses to decorate the new world.

Paul said the old Earth was ruined by sin, and it will be redeemed by Jesus' death, just as its inhabitants can also be redeemed (Rom 8:20–23). The death of Jesus means that God doesn't have to destroy humanity in order to remove sin, and he doesn't have to destroy the Earth in order to make it good again. Peter said the new Earth will be revealed when the old Earth is destroyed by fire, just as water destroyed civilization in Noah's day (2 Pet 3:5–13). This implies that the earth will be restored after the cleansing by fire, just as it was restored after the cleansing by a flood. Nowhere in the Bible is the new Earth portrayed as a replacement planet.

NEW EARTH

Tom Wright and other scholars have now reminded us that the Bible promises resurrection bodies and new life on a new earth—not in the heaven that we normally think of.[2] Although Revelation pictures the saints in heaven as "harpists harping on their harps" (Rev 14:2 KJV), this isn't their eternal occupation (as many of us will be glad to know). Revelation says believers are in heaven until the kingly Messiah initiates his rule on earth. At the end of the book, the church is envisioned as a city and a bride descending to the earth, which now has no ocean (21:1-2), and this presumably includes all those who had previously been kept safe in heaven (14:1-4, 13).

Even if God's renewal of the earth includes clearing up our mess, we should be looking after it for the sake of future generations, just as God asked previous generations to do for our sake. In the Old Testament God taught the Israelites how to be good stewards of their natural resources. Deuteronomy has a law against cutting down fruit trees even during wars: when the Israelites besieged a city, they were not to use fruit trees to make siege works (Deut 20:19-20). Fruit trees were the limited resources of that day.

God commanded the first humans to "increase in number; fill the earth and subdue it. Rule over … every living creature" (Gen 1:28). This is sometimes seen as an anti-ecology charter, and to some extent the wording supports this interpretation. The Hebrew *kabash* ("subdue") is normally used for defeated enemies or slaves. And the word *radah* ("rule") can imply a "ruthless" rule (Lev 25:46). It can even carry the sense of "asset stripping,"

---

2. Wright distills this well in *Surprised by Hope* (London: SPCK, 2007). See the useful review by Barry Seagren at BeThinking (TinyURL.com/SurpriseHope).

as in Judges 14:9, where Samson "scraped" the honey out of the lion's carcass.

However, God gave Adam a very different kind of command in the garden: there he was told to "work it and take care of it" (Gen 2:15). This translation doesn't quite express the nuance of the Hebrew. The word *avad* ("work") is normally translated "to serve" (as in the work of servants and priests), and *shamar* ("care for"/"keep") normally means "to guard, preserve" (as in Gen 3:24; 4:9) or "to obey, honor" (as in Gen 17:10; 18:19). In other words, Adam was asked to be the custodian of Eden, looking after it like a servant looks after his master's house or like a priest looks after a temple. It was only after the fall that Adam was told he'd have to subdue and rule nature, because outside Eden he had to do battle with weeds and carnivores.

LIKE EDEN

If we want the Earth to be more like Eden, then perhaps we should treat it in the way that God asked Adam to treat Eden. One day God will come in judgment to audit not only what we have done in our lives, but what we have done with his gifts. Jesus' parable of the wicked steward (Luke 16:1–9) suddenly has a very modern ring. His crime was wasting his master's resources, and his redemption came by planning for the future.

But this notion of a renewed new earth gives rise to a question: If this planet is going to be the home for our resurrected bodies, will it be big enough? And how will it last us for eternity? The Bible doesn't give us a full answer, but it does give us some clues.

Revelation suggests that we will live in a city, the new Jerusalem, that is even larger and more high-rise than New York: "The city was ... 12,000 stadia [about 1,400 miles] in length, and as wide and high as it is long" (Rev 21:16). This description reads like science fiction, but it may not be as fantastical as it sounds. Our atmosphere is only a few miles thick, and the international space station is only 220 miles above us, so the city cannot be 1,400 miles high, but perhaps it extends underground. (This might explain the mysterious details about the foundations in vv. 19-20—although this depth is beyond anything we can imagine building).

Whatever the actual shape of the city, it implies that people will live close to each other—and that they will love it. Perhaps in a sinless world, we will get along better. When Crocodile Dundee moved from his one-street Australian town to New York, with its population of six million people, he concluded they must be the friendliest people on Earth—because they'd all chosen to live close to each other! John has the same trusting and hopeful vision: a huge city filled with the redeemed from all of history, living peacefully together.

Cities get a bad reputation because many are poorly designed and most grow without careful planning. But John describes tree-lined waterways in this perfect city. And it has many gates—it isn't a prison—so presumably we'll be able to take trips around the restored Earth (Rev 21:12-14; 22:1-2).

Will there be enough room for us all in this city? Well, cities like Paris and Athens house about fifty thousand people per square mile. A few calculations show that even if the New Jerusalem has homes that are a hundred times larger than those in Paris, there would be room for a thousand times the total population that has ever lived on Earth until now (about 100 billion).[3] And if we all lived in this city, we'd still have a whole

---

3. Some ballpark calculations:

Paris has a population of 55,000 per square mile and Athens has 44,000 per square mile—so let's assume a rounded average of 48,000 per square mile. This includes public areas as well as homes.

natural planet to explore. I'm not concluding that the vision in Revelation is completely literal, but it isn't as impractical as one might first assume.

Does that mean we will all live on Earth forever? As things are now, that's clearly impossible because the fusion energy of the sun and the fission energy that heats the Earth's core will one day die out. However, the God who has planned things this far presumably has a plan for the longer term too.

Whether or not the new Earth is this planet, we should be planning for our future's children to be able to live here. Imagine if our grandparents' generation had decided to continuously heat their porches all night, so that if they felt like sitting outside at any time it would be nice and warm. If they'd done that, the oil and gas would have run out long before today. The ancient law that God gave Israel concerning fruit trees is a principle that

---

Now let's assume that in these cities an average building has three stories: some taller and some shorter; and some very tall ones that will compensate for large parks and roads, which are on a single level. So, the population living on a single level is 16,000 per square mile (48,000 ÷ 3).

The New Jerusalem is a cube measuring 12,000 stadia or 1,400 miles (Rev 21:16). If each floor is 20 feet high (i.e., twice as high as normal ceilings), the number of levels will be about 370,000 (1400 × 1760 × 3 ÷ 20 = 369,600).

Each level is 1400 × 1400 square miles. At a population density of 16,000 per square mile on each level, this allows for a total population of about 11,600 trillion (1400 × 1400 × 16,000 × 369,600 = 11,590,656,000,000,000).

If we give everyone a hundred times the average living space of someone in Paris, (i.e., everyone has a palace, and they also have access to a hundred times as much public space), this cuts the possible population to 116,000 billion.

The population of the planet throughout history has been about 107 billion. (See Wesley Stephenson, "Do the Dead Outnumber the Living?," BBC News, February 4, 2012 [TinyURL.com/DeadOutnumberLiving].) So there would be room for about one thousand times as many people who have ever lived, just in that city. This is if (and it is a huge "if") the description is meant at all literally.

he still wants us to follow: don't squander the next generation's inheritance.

SUMMARY

- Some Christians neglect conservation because there will be a "new Earth."

- The Bible says this is a restored planet, not a replacement, and we will live on it.

- Aspects of the envisioned new city of Jerusalem may be literal.

- *Proposal:* We should follow Old Testament guidelines to look after the planet and not squander its resources.

Section 3

▼

Adam and Eve

15

▾

Made from Dust, like Adam

The Bible tells us we are made of dust, and science tells us this dust was made in stars. Did God make Adam from dust in an afternoon or over billions of years? Science has a lot to say about this, but the best clue is in the Bible text.

As a child in Brighton I'd often visit the marina to explore the huge variety of boats, from fully rigged schooners to luxury yachts. My favorite discovery was a large catamaran called *Quasar* — a really cool name when this type of star-like object had only just been discovered. I heard that it was owned by one of the most hip and with-it people: Carl Sagan. Even if you've never heard of him, you'll know a saying he popularized: "We are all made of stardust."

Although this fact was discovered by an ardent atheist (Fred Hoyle, in 1954), this is important for all Christian apologists, because it helps explain why God made such a big universe.[1] All the interesting heavy atoms that are needed for life—such as carbon, iron, and phosphorus—are only made within larger stars.[2] When those stars die in a supernova explosion, these ele-

---

1. See chap. 3, "What Are the Stars For?"
2. See Ethan Siegel, "Going Nuclear: How Stars Die," Science Blogs, September 19, 2011 (TinyURL.com/HowStarsDie).

ments become interstellar dust. Gravity gradually draws this dust together to form new stars surrounded by planets made from these new elements that can support life. So life can't start until a whole generation of stars has lived and died, and a new generation of stars and planets has formed from the dust of dead stars.

In Genesis, all this occurs in the measureless time of the first verse, when God "created the heavens and the earth" (Gen 1:1). So the dust from which God made Adam was indeed star dust. Of course, the dust described in Genesis is "dust of the ground," not of the stars—though in reality this is the same because the planet is made of star dust. And the message is the same: whether the dust is described as coming from the ground or from the stars, the phrase tells us that we are made from "stuff"—elements of matter that God had already made.

ADAM MADE FROM DUST

When Genesis says that God made Adam from "dust," we should regard this as a very bold claim. I can point to bookshelves I've made, but I have to admit I used a self-assembly kit. A carpenter could claim to make them "from scratch"—though what he means is planks and screws. This claim would be more accurate if someone was shipwrecked on an island, so he had to cut down trees and smelt iron ore that he found. And someone who grew the trees from seeds and dug up ore from deep mines could claim to make the shelves "from seeds and soil." Of course, no human could make the further claim that they made the seeds and induced volcanoes to bring up iron from the planet's core. But God can claim even more than that: he made the planet itself because he is responsible for making the stars that exploded into planet-forming dust. He is the only one who can claim to make things "from dust."

What is it, then, that Genesis is describing when it says that "God formed a man from the dust of the ground" (Gen 2:7)? Does it describe God taking elements from the soil and building a human in a single day? The text says that God started when "no shrub had yet appeared on the earth and no plant had yet sprung up. ... Then the Lord God formed a man" (Gen 2:5–7). If we try to line this up with chapter 1, God must have started before day three, when plants appeared. However, the account in chapter 2 may not be as chronological as chapter 1, so conclusions are difficult. It may also mean that God gradually made man from dust over millions of years using evolution to produce simple life, then complex life, and finally a human. The text itself could mean either, so how do we decide the correct interpretation?

EVERYONE MADE FROM DUST

A significant clue about the meaning of "dust" comes from the Bible itself, because the same concept is used with regard to all of us—we are *all* made from dust. Later authors say: "You molded me like clay. Will you now turn me to dust again?"; "All come from dust, and to dust all return"; "The dust returns to the ground it came from, and the spirit returns to God who gave it" (Job 10:9; Eccl 3:20; 12:7). Notice that the Bible adds the sobering thought that we will also return to dust, and this is repeated again elsewhere (Job 34:15; Pss 90:3; 104:29).

In what way are *we*, as individuals, made from dust? God doesn't fashion us from the soil in our parents' garden—he shapes us all individually from the genetic inheritance of our parents and the nourishment they lovingly give us. We grow by eating dust—that is, the matter in animals and in plants that grows from dust. And our bodies are made of dust—that is, the same elements of matter that Adam's body was made from. We inherit some of that dust as the patterns in Adam's DNA—that very special and intricate matter that was passed down over thousands of years from Adam and through our parents. So when the Bible says *we* are made of dust, this dust must refer to Adam's genes and the elements that both we and he are made from.

Therefore, when the Bible says that God made us from dust, this implies a long process through countless generations from Adam. And when it says that God made Adam from dust, it can mean the same thing. That is, he made Adam from a genetic inheritance that he had already prepared for him through countless preceding generations. All humans, including Adam, are made from dust in the same way—by inheriting information passed on in matter and by eating matter consisting of elements that were made from star dust.

This implies that God started the process of making Adam from dust long before he made Eden or any part of planet Earth. The dust that Adam was made from had to first be made inside stars—so, as far back as the appearance of the first stars, God was thinking of us.

MORE THAN DUST

A significant phrase occurs just after "dust" in Genesis 2:7: God "breathed into his nostrils the breath of life." Genesis has already said that God made Adam just like he made other animals—from the dust—so Adam was already alive in the sense that all animals are alive. Then Genesis informs us that God made humans into something very special with his very own "breath of life." It is possible that this simply means that Adam started breathing, but that would be true of all animals. It is more likely to refer to God breathing "spirit" into Adam. The Bible refers to spirit in humans but not in animals, and it appears to be this spirit that makes humans able to be aware of God and able to communicate with him.[3]

God giving Adam a spirit is the climax of the glorious message of Genesis. It provides a reason why humans are the final purpose and aim of creation in Genesis. We are the species with whom God shares his Spirit and with whom he communicates spiritually.

God didn't make just us and the planet we live on; he also created the whole universe to be our planet's womb. In order to make humans, he started by creating a universe with enough galaxies to continue existing long enough for generations of stars to glow, to die, to explode, and to re-form with planets made of complex elements. On one of those planets God could make life. The message of Genesis is that the whole of creation was part of God's plan to make *us*.

Science can never discover the reason or purpose behind the universe, so God has had to reveal this to us by other means: the Bible. He spent so much time lovingly creating our home planet and then, when the planet was full of life, he revealed himself by joining us briefly as a human, knowing that most of us would reject him. We don't just happen to be made from star dust: we have been made from star dust *by* God, and *for* a purpose.

---

3. See chap. 17, "What Does the Human Spirit Do?"

SUMMARY

- God made not only Adam but also the star dust he was made from.

- Adam was made of more than just dust: God breathed into him (Gen 2:7).

- All humans are "made of dust" (Job 10:9; Ps 90:3; etc.), molded through generations of ancestors.

- *Proposal:* Adam was made from dust like all humans—molded through generations of ancestors—and became the first human when God breathed into him.

16

▾

Animals Have Souls in the Bible

Some animals can use tools, show emotions, and communicate with words, so are humans merely clever animals? The Bible and psychologists use different language but agree on this distinction: humans are spiritual, while animals have only souls.

If you've ever had a dog or cat, there won't be any doubt in your mind that animals have emotions and thoughts very similar to humans. They can be happy, sad, excited, cross, and even mournful when someone dies. They can also anticipate the future: they get excited when you put on your shoes and pick up their leash. And they have curiosity: even when a new object clearly can't be eaten and is too small to urinate on, they will nonetheless investigate it. An abundance of YouTube videos show abashed-looking dogs trying to hide their misdeeds, which testifies that they can deliberately do something that they know is wrong and be concerned about it.

Does this suggest that humans are really nothing more than clever animals? After all, it seems that the only obvious difference between us and other animals is the sophistication of our language. If animals could speak (an idea explored widely in fiction), would they be virtually identical to us?

Surprisingly, the Bible seems to concur with this view, because it describes both humans and animals as having something very significant in common: a "soul." The Bible uses the word "soul" frequently with regard to animals, so the traits listed above could be viewed as the qualities shared by all creatures that have a soul. On the other hand, the Bible also implies that humans are very different from animals because it says that humans are the only animals that have a "spirit."

SOUL AND SPIRIT

Outside the Bible, it isn't common for a distinction to be made between the terms "soul" and "spirit," but the Bible differentiates between them in a remarkably consistent way. The words for "soul" (Hebrew *nephesh* and Greek *psuchē*) are always used only for animals and humans and never for God or angels. In contrast, the words for "spirit" (Hebrew *ruach* and Greek *pneuma*) are used only for humans, God, and angels. Actually, there is *one* exception, in Ecclesiastes 3:21—the only one out of 1,655 occurrences of these words—where the word "spirit" is used of an animal. However, since this was probably quoting a well-known proverb of the time, it doesn't really express the theology of the Bible.

The Bible doesn't define the difference between a soul and a spirit, though we can learn a lot from the way that it uses these words.[1] In this chapter, we will try to discover what "soul" means, and in the next we will look more carefully at "spirit." The Bible implies that we are similar to animals because we have a soul, but dissimilar because we also have a spirit. It seems that a soul is what distinguishes animals from plants and rocks, while

---

1. For all the instances of "soul" and "spirit" (and the different ways they are translated into English) using STEPBible.org, go to TinyURL.com/SoulOT; TinyURL.com/SoulNT; TinyURL.com/STEP-SpiritOT; TinyURL.com/SpiritNT. There's another potential exception in Gen 7:22, where (translating word-by-word) "all which [have] breath [of] spirit [of] life in their nostrils" either means all living things, or it expresses the tragedy that this included spiritual beings— i.e., humans.

a spirit is what distinguishes us from animals—it encapsulates the essence of humanity. This suggests that we can find out what a soul is by looking at features we share with animals.

LANGUAGE AND EMPATHY

Social biologists have been struggling for decades with various theories about what makes us unique from animals. Most of these theories have been disproved one by one as they have made new discoveries about the actual lifestyles and amazing abilities of various animals.

We now know, for instance, that several animals can use tools—chimps use a stick to reach food, and crows will even bend a wire to a shape that reaches into corners better. And although animals are mostly afraid of fire, they can overcome this—bonobo apes have even learned to light a match to warm a marshmallow (a treat they enjoy as much as we do). Social animals will help each other even if they aren't related—a rat will let himself get wet to help a friend stay dry. Chimps have a strong sense of justice—they'll even refuse a reward of food, seemingly on a matter of principle, if they see another chimp being given a better reward than theirs. And yet they'll also steal food, although they are careful to do this only when the theft won't be detected by a more powerful chimp. Unlike humans, no animals have verbal skills, though one bonobo ape has learned to understand the meaning of a few thousand different verbal words and can communicate by pointing to a vocabulary of five hundred symbols. Even in the wild, at least sixty-six distinct gestures so far have been identified as being used by chimps.[2]

---

2. These examples and more are at Melissa Hogenboom, "Humans Are Nowhere Near as Special as We Like to Think," BBC Earth, July 3, 2015 (TinyURL. com/LessUnique); and Alexandra Michel, "Humans Are Animals, Too: A

As we've seen, animals can display their own feelings, but they can also recognize emotions in others—chimps, for example, react differently to each other in circumstances that might indicate the other animal is angry or sad. To some extent, they can even identify each other's emotions from facial expressions. We are familiar with recognizing when our pets are happy or sad, but animal psychologists have found that animals experience a wide range of other emotions, ranging from fear of anticipated events to mourning following bereavement.

There are some things that animals can't do. For instance, unlike even a young child, they can't work out what another individual believes. Psychologists test this ability in children by using the Sally–Anne test.[3] The child is shown a doll, Sally, who puts a marble in a box while another doll, Anne, is watching. Sally is then taken out of the room, and the doll Anne takes the marble from the box and puts it in a basket. When Sally is brought back into the room, the psychologist asks the child: "Where will Sally look for the marble?" From about the age of four, children know that Sally will look in the box because that's where she *believes* the marble is. That is, the child can distinguish between what is true and what someone else *believes* is true.

This suggests one ability in humans that may be related to the presence of a spirit—our ability to empathize. A well-trained artificial intelligence (AI) can work out what emotion someone is feeling from their expression, but humans can do this from much smaller cues and sometimes from none, except that they know what they *would* feel. This is as close as we get to telepathy, and it almost seems like we can read each other's minds.

Whirlwind Tour of Cognitive Biology," Association for Psychological Science, April 28, 2017 (TinyURL.com/HumanCogBiol).

   3.   See Wikipedia, "Sally–Anne test" (TinyURL.com/SallyAnneTest).

Another thing no other animals can handle is the grammar of language. This is so natural to humans that we don't realize we are doing it. But when someone tries to explain how English verbs conjugate (and what this means), we realize that this easy task is actually quite complex. Human brains are hardwired to learn how to string verbs, nouns, and adjectives together, and we quickly learn to construct complex sentences.

My daughter said her first sentence just before her second birthday, when I asked her where the eraser on the end of her pencil had gone. Thinking about every word carefully, and evidently aware that she had to place them in the correct order, she pointed at the disc drive in the side of my laptop and said, "In the hole." The repair was expensive, but I couldn't be angry with her! Some chimps and apes can learn an impressive vocabulary, but they can't do anything more complex than link words together in a random order.

LEARNING AND TEACHING

Recent work with animals suggests that they also learn in a different way from humans. Like humans, many animals copy each other, both to learn useful activities such as using tools or by imitating the best courtship displays in order to win a better mate. And they also copy each other in doing seemingly *non*-useful things. For instance, when some dolphins in captivity were taught to water-walk, after they were released into the wild other dolphins copied them doing this.[4] But unlike humans, animals don't appear to spend time specifically *teaching* each

---

4. See "Dolphins Learn from Each Other to Walk on Water," University of St Andrews, August 29, 2018 (TinyURL.com/DolphinWalk).

other—skills are merely passed on by being observed and copied.[5]

One of the first jobs Adam had was teaching. First, he was asked to name all the animals (Gen 2:19)—perhaps a reference to language development—and later he had to teach Eve the important instructions that God had given him. She was created after God had told Adam: "You must not eat from the tree of the knowledge of good and evil, for when you eat from it you will certainly die" (Gen 2:17), so presumably it was his task to teach her about this vital aspect of life in the garden. When Eve had that fatal conversation with Satan in the form of a snake, she clearly knew about the command, but the version she quoted to him was subtly different: "You must not eat fruit from the tree that is in the middle of the garden, *and you must not touch it*, or you will die" (Gen 3:3). The words in italics weren't recorded as part of God's message to Adam.

Did Eve embellish it, or did Adam exaggerate? I suspect it was the latter because it sounds like something an adult says to a child: "Don't turn the knobs on the stove—in fact, don't even touch them!" The rabbis spotted a potential consequence of Adam's exaggeration: they suggested that Satan deliberately "nudged" Eve against the tree, and when she didn't die, it caused her to doubt what God had said. She had been taught that she'd die if she touched it, which had been proved false. This left her open to the suggestion that eating the fruit wouldn't be harmful

---

5.   Meerkats may be a rare exception. See Weird Animal Questions of the Week, "Schooled: Animals That Teach Their Young," *National Geographic* (TinyURL.com/MeerkatsTeach). But humans are truly distinctive in their dedication to long-term teaching through culture as well as language. See Kevin Laland, "What Made Us Unique," *Scientific American* (September 2018) (TinyURL. com/DifferentAnimal).

either. Clearly the art of teaching is also something that needs to be taught.[6]

However, these abilities that humans alone have—teaching, language skills, or working out what others believe—are not the uniqueness of humans encapsulated in what the Bible calls the "spirit." After all, AI systems can be programmed to teach, and although they are taught how to do this by humans, they are still doing something that no animal can do. Some AIs are now so flawless at spoken English, including human-like pauses and filler words such as "um," that new laws are proposed that will require them to announce their nonhuman identity when making phone calls. AI artists are certainly better than I am at copying reality, and now they can even invent realistic scenes and faces; additionally, AI music programs can now create novel tunes and orchestration. (The robot that makes me feel personally inadequate is the one that can construct IKEA furniture—though I think the developers cheated by rewriting the instructions.) So although these activities cannot be done by animals, they can't be regarded as the essence of humanity.

WORSHIP AND PRAYER

What really makes humans unique is that they worship and pray. No animals appear to do anything like this—we never see them giving honor to objects or images, or any ritualistic behavior directed to an individual they can't see. Animals do take part in social-bonding activities that have no apparent purpose, and they may show obeisance to an alpha male, but they don't seem to be interested in anything beyond their world of physical senses.

In contrast, human children appear to be naturally religious. They tend to attribute purpose to aspects of nature that they

---

6. See Genesis Rabbah 19:3–4 (TinyURL.com/GenRabbah19).

observe, as though it was created or designed by a higher being. When six-year-olds are asked why birds exist, they say things like "to make nice music."[7] This doesn't necessarily mean that we are born with a knowledge of God, but it does mean we are born with the propensity to expect a creator to exist. This continues into adulthood as a belief that things must happen "for a reason"—a belief that even atheists find difficult to dispel when something bad happens to them.

Child psychologists have also noted that children like to pray, even when their parents disapprove. There isn't (yet) any evidence that children have an innate wish or ability to pray to God, but once they are taught that this is a possibility, they are keen to join in or pray by themselves. And if they are discouraged, they often still want to continue this practice. I remember a sad anecdote in a book on developmental psychology: a pair of young sisters knew that their mother didn't approve of praying, so they waited until she'd said goodnight and left them alone before praying quietly together. Psychologists clearly can't confirm that God hears such prayers, but they have found that there is a statistically beneficial effect for children who pray because they develop healthy approaches to life and cope well in crises.[8]

I doubt that we will ever be able to prove or disprove that prayer is an innate human activity. It would require bringing up some children in isolation so that they never come across the concept—an experiment that would be ruled out by any ethics

---

7. See the summary of Justin Barrett's work at the *Telegraph*, "Children Are Born Believers in God, Academic Claims," *Telegraph*, November 14, 2008 (TinyURL.com/BarrettChildrenGod), and his summary of similar work by others at the *Guardian*, "Let's Stick to the Science," *Guardian*, November 29, 2008 (TinyURL.com/BarrettChildren).

8. See Vivienne Mountain, "Prayer Is a Positive Activity for Children," *International Journal of Children's Spirituality* 10 (2005): 3 (TinyURL.com/ChildrenPrayer).

committee. However, prayer and worship appear to be universal in human societies. Every isolated tribe discovered by missionaries, and the few isolated tribes still in existence, all have some kind of religion that includes a wish to communicate with a higher being.

For the last couple of centuries, people have theorized that religion would wane and eventually diminish until the number of people who had religious beliefs would be as small as those who believe in a flat earth. However, belief in the supernatural has persisted throughout the world, and the decline of established religions has merely been replaced by simpler types of religion such as belief in the power of crystals, lucky numbers, karma, or horoscopes. Atheism is certainly more common than it used to be, but true atheists are still rare.[9] The recent popularity of conspiracy theories may be a kind of religion substitute because these usually envisage a higher power invisibly at work, such as a secret human agency or aliens, and a belief that you can cope better with life if you know about them. Such beliefs appeal to the same tendency of humans to look for a cause behind apparently random events and to search for someone who is in control.

We have to conclude that our pets are more similar to us than we like to admit. Very few activities are unique to our species, and some of these—such as speech and morality—may be merely due to our larger brains. However, there are two ways in which humans are different: they take time to teach each other, and they attempt to discover and communicate with a deity or

---

9. In 2010, 84 percent of the world's population were still affiliated with an official religion. See "The Global Religious Landscape," Pew Research Center, December 18, 2012 (TinyURL.com/84PC-Religious).

other unseen forces. So the Bible appears to be right that we have an animal "soul," but we also have a "spirit."

Science is helping us to understand more about an intriguing fact about humans: that we are significantly different from animals by being spiritual. We'll explore this more in the next chapter, but one very significant factor stands out in the Bible: we share our possession of a spirit with angels and God himself. It is clearly a very important and elevating part of our makeup that potentially allows us into the presence of God—both now and for eternity.

SUMMARY

- Animals use tools, show emotions, and communicate with primitive language.

- The Bible uses "soul" for animals as well as for humans, which may acknowledge these emotions and abilities.

- The Bible does not use "spirit" when referring to animals.

- *Proposal:* Our "spirit" is what enables us to communicate with God, and it helps us show more empathy and cooperation.

17

▾

What Does the Human Spirit Do?

What is the difference between the human spirit and soul? Neu-rologists and philosophers ask a similar question about the mind and brain.

A bizarre experiment took place in 1907 when an American doctor, Duncan MacDougall, tried to measure the weight of the human spirit. He put the beds of six dying men on an industrial weighing machine and found that one of them lost three-quarters of an ounce when he died. The other five results gave the "wrong" answer, so they were dismissed as faulty. You won't be surprised to hear that more accurate equipment under controlled conditions has failed to replicate this experiment.[1]

Almost all human functions can now be traced to physical impulses from the brain, hormones, social interactions, and learning. In the previous chapter we saw that very few abilities are unique to our species, and some of these are merely due to our larger brains. That's why the Bible speaks of a "soul" (our emotions, personality, and life) as residing in animals as well as humans. But the Bible also refers to another component that is separate from our bodies—our "spirit"—and it uses the words

---

1. See Wikipedia, "21 Grams Experiment" (TinyURL.com/21GramSpirit).

for "spirit" only with regard to God, angels, and humans, but not animals.

The Bible uses "soul" (Hebrew *nephesh* and Greek *psuchē*) as a word for part of the body. It is used when counting numbers, because the soul is part of the visible body (e.g., Gen 46:18, 22, 25, 26, 27, where each number is followed in the Hebrew by "souls"). It is even used when "soul" means a corpse—for example, in the laws about touching a dead person (Num 5:2; 6:6, 11; 9:6, 7, 10; 19:11, 13). In contrast, a "spirit" (Hebrew *ruach* and Greek *pneuma*) is described as something that isn't seen and can't be grasped in your hand—like the wind (John 3:8).

SPIRIT AND BODY

The Bible regards the spirit as being within the body but not part of it. While a fetus is growing, "the spirit comes to the bones in the womb" (Eccl 11:5 ESV) just as God originally "formed the spirit of man within him" (Zech 12:1 ESV). Then, at death, "the spirit returns to God who gave it" (Eccl 12:7): so the psalmist says, "into your hands I commit my spirit" (Ps 31:5)—which Jesus quoted when he "gave up his spirit" (Matt 27:50; Luke 23:46; John 19:30)—and Stephen said, "Receive my spirit" (Acts 7:59). When someone was brought back from death, "her spirit returned" (Luke 8:55). After death, the flesh is destroyed, but the "spirit" survives (1 Cor 5:5; 1 Pet 3:18), and God determines how good this spirit is (Prov 16:2)—though the "spirits" of believers are made righteous by God himself (Heb 12:23). It appears, therefore, that a human spirit can live without a body, but a body without a spirit is dead (Jas 2:26). However, we are promised a new body for our spirits (1 Cor 15:35–49), like Jesus, who rose with his new body as the "firstborn from among dead" (Col 1:18; Rev 1:5). He was not merely a spirit because "a spirit does not have flesh and bones as you see that I have" (Luke 24:39 ESV).

The Bible also describes the spirit as the part of us that makes decisions. When God caused someone to be obstinate, God made his "spirit" stubborn (Deut 2:30), and people have "no spirit left" (Josh 2:11 ESV) in situations of extreme fear and helplessness (Josh 5:1; Ps 142:3). When tempted, "the spirit is willing," but "the flesh is weak" (Mark 14:38 = Matt 26:41). God "stirred up the spirit of Cyrus king of Persia" to make him decide to release Israel from their exile (2 Chr 36:22; Ezra 1:1 ESV), then stirred the spirits of individual Jews to go and rebuild the Temple (Ezra 1:5; Hag 1:14). When humans rebel against God, it is their "spirit" that turns against him (Job 15:13 ESV; Ps 78:8), and when they decide to follow him they are "contrite ... in spirit" (Isa 57:15; 66:2; also 1 John 4:3). It is the "spirit" that is born again and renewed when someone turns to God (John 3:6; Ps 51:10; Ezek 11:19; 18:31; 36:26).

SPIRITS COMMUNICATE

We communicate with God through the Holy Spirit, who speaks to our spirit and teaches our spirit how to pray (Rom 8:16, 27; 1 Cor 14:14), because these things are "spiritually discerned" (1 Cor 2:14 ESV). We can pray with our minds, but this is different from praying with our spirit (1 Cor 14:15). Only a person's own spirit really knows their inner thoughts—other than God himself (1 Cor 2:11).

Therefore, "spirit" is not just another word for "soul." Paul makes it very clear that they are different when he refers to our "whole spirit, soul and body" (1 Thess 5:23; also Heb 4:12). The soul is part of the human body (and part of an animal's body), whereas a spirit can exist independently of the body, though it may feel somewhat naked till it can "clothe itself with the imperishable"—the new body (1 Cor 15:50–54).

One way to think about our spirit is to imagine trying to connect to the internet. Our brain is like a computer suffused with the information signals from the internet, but we can't read any-thing online or talk to anyone with it unless we have a router to communicate. Our spirit can intercept and understand things on a spiritual level, which we may be completely unaware of even with our minds. Likewise, an animal can't communicate on a spiritual level because it doesn't have a spirit and isn't even aware that anything exists to communicate with.

And to take the analogy further, a computer connected to the internet only becomes useful when we have a keyboard to interact with it. Without that, the computer would just be inac-tive, waiting for instructions, and we wouldn't be aware that it was connected to the internet. This implies that having a spirit is not enough: there must be some component in our brain that acts like that keyboard for interacting with it. This suggests that even if an ape had a spirit, the ape's brain wouldn't be able to connect with it. But our brains have developed differently, so that when God implanted a spirit in humans, our brains *were* able to interact with it—though we don't yet know how. The result is that we are no longer just animals interacting with the physical world; we are also open to the whole spiritual world—whether we take time to explore it or not.

What is it in our brains that is different—that allows us to connect on a spiritual level? We cannot answer this question because it is difficult for any kind of science to investigate some-thing that is completely immaterial; by its nature, our spirit will not interact with any instruments or photographic chemicals.

What about interactions in the other direction, from our spirit to our body? If a spirit can't interact with matter, then it can't move a limb, or influence emotions via chemicals (such as adrenaline), or create even the merest spark of thought in the brain. If it cannot interact with anything physical, it can only observe. Our human bodies would get on with life by means of animal reflexes: eating, growing, having temper tantrums, learning to speak, having children, getting ill, and dying. If our spirit cannot interact with the brain, it can never prompt us to do anything "spiritual," or even to show kindness to someone; we would merely act like clever animals, and our spirit would be a voiceless onlooker.

This problem is related to that of free will: we all *feel* as though we can freely make moral decisions, many of us *feel* as though we can communicate with God, and almost all of us *feel* as though we are a "person" who should be able to survive death—but this might all be an illusion. Theologians talk about the spirit, while philosophers and neuroscientists talk about the mind, but neither has any way to describe it in a way that can be tested. On their own, neither the Bible nor science helps us to define or discover what a spirit or mind is. However, together, the two areas of knowledge may bring us a little closer to doing so.

The various sciences have led us to regard the world like a complex billiard table, where hitting one ball inevitably results in movements by other balls in a predictable way. In that case, if we had a computer big enough to record the position and movement of every atom, then in theory we could predict exactly what would happen at any point in the future. Just as we can wind forward the mechanism of a planetarium to see when the next solar eclipse will happen, we could theoretically examine a person and the whole world around them to predict when he would next lose their temper.

QUANTUM CONNECTION

However, this is only true up to a certain point because predictability doesn't extend to the subatomic world, where quantum uncertainty takes over. On a billiard table we can measure exactly where a stationary ball is, but if it were as small as an electron we'd only be able to measure its stationary position to the nearest 10^{-35} meters.[2] This Heisenberg uncertainty principle is not due to the limitations of our measuring instruments but is part of the fundamental nature of matter itself. It means that when, for example, two neutrons collide, one of them may split into a proton and electron, or it may not—and it is impossible to predict with certainty whether it will happen even under identical circumstances. When this uncertainty was first discovered, there were many skeptics—including Albert Einstein—but all the experiments at institutions such as the CERN (the European Organization for Nuclear Research) continue to confirm it.

Quantum uncertainty does not mean that the universe is unpredictable, because these uncertainties only occur at the subatomic level and average themselves out at larger scales. These tiny particles are like mayflies hovering over a lake. They could conceivably cause a ripple in the water if they all gathered in one small spot and all flew in the same direction, but because they all fly randomly in different directions, their movements cancel each other out. However, this tiny area of uncertainty may also be influenced by spiritual forces in ways we don't understand and can't measure. Of course, we can't know this for certain, but we also can't rule it out.

Academics have seriously considered the possibility that our spirit could interact with our brains at the quantum level, below the threshold of quantum uncertainty. For example, Peter Clarke, a neurologist who happens to be a Christian, has done the math to see whether this would allow the spirit to fire an individual neuron. Unfortunately, the calculations don't add up: the amount of action that could be performed in this tiny

---

2. See chap. 2, "God *Does* Work in the Gaps."

area of unpredictability is not enough to make even a single neuron fire.[3] This is an ongoing area of research, and Clarke has indicated some currently insurmountable problems, though he didn't take into account cascade reactions, where tiny causes can result in larger effects. Quantum effects have now been found to trigger our sense of smell, which makes it more reasonable that quantum fluctuations may trigger thoughts, too; however, this kind of research is in its infancy.[4]

NO CONFLICT

It is therefore reasonable to suppose that an immaterial spirit, which cannot be measured or contained, can nevertheless interact with human thought without being detectable by any possible machine or other person. That is, although we cannot yet demonstrate this, it is not contrary to reason or to what we do already know. Our spirit may indeed act as a "ghost in the machine" by making decisions that are communicated to our brain and thereby turned into thought and action. Of course, I am not concluding that this is definitely the way that a spirit inhabits and influences a body. At present we can only conclude that it *could* be, though this is sufficient to show that there is no necessary conflict between the science of neurology, the philosophy of mind, and the theology of an immaterial human spirit.

This spirit enables us to know that there is something "out there" that we can communicate with. Returning to the analogy of our spirit being like a router installed in our computer brain, prayer is like a computer microphone to enable communication with God. Most of us don't have anything equivalent to a screen

---

3. Peter G. H. Clarke, "Determinism, Brain Function and Free Will," *Science and Christian Belief* 22 (2010) (TinyURL.com/ClarkeFreeWill).

4. See Jason Palmer, "'Quantum Smell' Idea Gains Ground," BBC News, January 28, 2013 (TinyURL.com/SmellQuantum).

or headphones on this equipment because we don't see visions of God or hear his voice. However, that we aren't conscious of hearing him in the same way that we hear from other people doesn't mean that we don't hear him at all. Most of what happens in our brains occurs subconsciously, so why should our interactions with God be any different? Just as some people can learn to control their heart rate (which is normally done subconsciously), some individuals (called "prophets" in the Bible) are able to audibly hear and sometimes see things from God.

One result of having a spirit is that God's Holy Spirit can interact with us. This makes us truly different from animals, and explains why humans are alone in their wish to worship and pray to God. It also helps to explain why every one of us is so important to him.

SUMMARY

- The Bible uses "spirit" for the nonphysical part of us that communicates with God.

- In that case, our physical brain has to interact with something instruments can't measure.

- Biological functions such as smell occur as quantum-level interactions.

- **Proposal:** The brain and spirit may interact at a level of quantum uncertainty.

18

▼

Adam's Apple in Literal Language

When the account of Eden's ribs, snakes, and trees is expressed in modern concepts, it agrees surprisingly well with the literal text. Gerontologists would love to know what grew on the tree of life.

Fruit is good for you—unless it's the only forbidden fruit on the planet. One bite of this, and the whole human race suffered. Most attempts to depict the story of the garden of Eden in Genesis 3 look embarrassingly silly; inevitably, it seems, we end up with images in our minds of strategically placed foliage and sly-looking snakes. And why did God put the dangerous forbidden fruit so temptingly on display? Was he trying to catch Adam and Eve out? It seems like leaving a tin of sweets within your children's reach and telling them not to eat any while you're out of the room. This whole description of a protected paradise with two special trees, a talking animal, and everlasting gardening suggests that it might be a parable about temptation rather than an account of early human history.

Personally, I prefer to regard Bible narratives as accounts of actual events whenever possible, so I'm going to see how far I can get with that. I don't mean that it shouldn't or can't be a metaphorical or poetic story about how sin or death came to humanity, but before deciding that's the case, we should try to understand the narrative literally. We may, of course, have to update the language a little, because the ancient audience for whom Genesis was written had no terminology for subjects such as cloning, genetics, or the biological causes of aging, so the original account couldn't refer to such concepts. Here's an attempt at rewriting the narrative of Genesis 3 as it might have been written if its first readers had lived in the twenty-first century:

MODERN RETELLING OF GENESIS 3

God selected one of the upright, large-brained, human-looking animals that he had slowly and lovingly nurtured from the dust of exploded stars over billions of years and gave that animal a spirit. This transformed the human animal into a human being who was capable of communicating with God. His spirit also enabled the man to think about the future and to make voluntary moral decisions.

This first human being lived in Eden—an area of fertile land enclosed by a wall that protected him from harm. This protection was necessary because in order to produce harmony in the good and perfect world, all other living things experienced a life cycle involving reproduction and death. Life cycles are implicit in the seasons of autumn and spring, the eating of plants and smaller animals by larger animals, and adaptation to new environments by having offspring with new abilities. Eden was special because human death was prevented. The garden boundary kept out carcinogens, dangerous animals, and all other sources of harm; inside there was healthy food and useful plants that needed tending.

Because God wanted human beings to live forever, he had selected one with healthy genes and no diseases that he might pass on. God then took some of the man's tissue and made a kind of clone who was identical to him except for the lack of his Y chromosome, so she was female. To prevent them from aging, God provided a "tree of life"—a source of life-preserving supplements that kept them alive as long as they ingested them regularly. When they multiplied to "fill the earth," they would be able to make copies of that tree and extend the boundary of the garden. However, exclusion from the garden would deny them access to this tree, so they would start to die.

This description of the creation of the first human beings has certainly lost the poetic beauty of the ancient text, but it helps us to recognize that it could be describing an actual set of events. Previous generations wouldn't have understood the language I have used here, and we may not understand a similar account that is made in a hundred years' time. Perhaps, by then, everyone will know a word for the type of substances that the tree of life provided for preventing human death.

PREVENTING AGING

Gerontology is a new medical discipline that deals mainly with the various disabilities of aging, but it is starting to make some progress in preventing the causes of aging.[1] There is still little consensus or definite progress in this area, but even without a breakthrough, more than half the babies now born in the West are expected to live to a hundred years.[2] At present, most people are still dying of diseases, accidents, infections, degradation of organs such as the heart, liver, brain, and so on, and uncontrollable cell division (i.e., cancer). However, as medicine improves,

---

1. For a summary of various theories, see João Pedro de Magalhães, "Damage-Based Theories of Aging," Senescence (TinyURL.com/AgingCauses).

2. See Datablog, "How Many People Will Live to 100 in Developed Countries?," *Guardian*, May 7, 2017 (TinyURL.com/LiveToCentury).

more of us are dying of "old age"—which, intriguingly, is written into our genes.

Throughout our lives, almost every part of our body is continuously regenerating itself, except for our reproductive cells (eggs and sperm) and the lenses in our eyes, which harden in our forties and eventually turn into useless cataracts.[3] However, we have a built-in age limit because eventually the rest of our cells also stop dividing and repairing. The ends of each human chromosome in our cells are capped with a telomere—a short code sequence that is repeated about twenty-five hundred times. When a cell ages, it divides to produce two youthful cells, but during this process it loses about ten of these code sequences, so the telomere cap shortens. When it gets too short, the cell cannot divide and becomes senescent—that is, it grows old and slows down. Tantalizingly, a hormone called telomerase can regenerate the telomeres, but this only works in reproductive cells, and no one has found a way to make it work elsewhere.[4] Of course, its use might increase the rate of cancers, but reproductive cells have an answer for that: they have extremely active DNA-repair mechanisms that are almost foolproof.[5] So, if things are as simple as we hope (and they rarely are), humans have an inbuilt mechanism for extending our life almost indefinitely, but we haven't worked out how to activate it yet. Perhaps it is merely a matter of identifying the food supplement that was in the tree of life.

There are some details in Genesis that are more difficult to retell in scientific terms, such as the snake and the other special

---

3. See "How Quickly Do Different Cells in the Body Replace Themselves?," Cell Biology by the Numbers (TinyURL.com/CellsReplace).

4. See Wikipedia, "Telomere" (TinyURL.com/WikiTelomeres).

5. See Wikipedia, "DNA Repair" (TinyURL.com/WikiRepairDNA) and Suzanne Clancy, "DNA Damage & Repair: Mechanisms for Maintaining DNA Integrity," *Nature Education* 1 (2008): 103 (TinyURL.com/DamagedDNA).

tree—the forbidden "tree of the knowledge of good and evil."
For this, we have to change to the language of another specialist
area of knowledge—that is, we have to use theological language:

> *The first two human beings, like us, had the ability to make*
> *moral choices, although there was little to tempt them to do*
> *wrong because they felt no danger, had no needs, and had no*
> *rivals. However, their free will could lead them into rebelling*
> *against God. So God included a minor prohibition that would*
> *act as an early warning signal that they were starting to rebel.*
> *He told them that they should not eat from one particular*
> *tree—the "tree of the knowledge of good and evil." This tree*
> *didn't actually transfer any knowledge, but the act of eating*
> *from it conveyed the knowledge that they could—and did—*
> *disobey God. That is, this action informed them that it was*
> *possible to do evil as well as good. If they could do this, they*
> *could also harm animals or even harm each other. They were*
> *expelled from the garden in order that the evil each one did*
> *would be confined to one lifetime.*

THE SPREADING OF DEATH

Death didn't come immediately when Adam and Eve were
expelled. Their ideal genes gave them and their descendants a
lifespan of hundreds of years. This is perhaps confirmed by the
extraordinary lifespans of kings in the Sumerian lists before the
time of the flood.[6] By the time of Abraham, the human lifespan
had gradually reduced to 175 years (Gen 25:7), and soon after it
settled down to an average of about seventy years (Ps 90:10).
Adam was responsible for bringing death to the whole human

---

6. See Wikipedia, "Sumerian King List" (TinyURL.com/SumerianKings).

race because his sin meant that we no longer lived in Eden, where humans could eat from the tree of life and live forever. Romans 5:12 says that Adam introduced "death," and that this spread "to all people, because all sinned." So Adam doesn't bear all the guilt, because we ourselves also sin.

Did Adam's sin also bring death to plants, animals, and bacteria? The only indication that this may have happened is in Romans 8: "Creation was subjected to frustration, not by its own choice, but by the will of the one who subjected it, in hope that the creation itself will be liberated from its bondage to decay and brought into the freedom and glory of the children of God" (8:20-21). However, this doesn't say that death was absent before Adam. What this passage *does* say is that the creation suffers "decay" (*phthora*, which implies death) but also "frustration" (*mataiotēs*, which has the sense of "meaninglessness" and "emptiness") until "the children of God" experience "freedom and glory." This "frustration" is a good description of the meaninglessness of death and decay *after* the entrance of sin into the world.

Plant and animal death had always been a necessary and natural aspect of lifecycles in creation. Death results in seasons, rejuvenation, and adaptive change, which are all "good" features of creation—so long as there is a purpose. But when creation lost its purpose (when Adam stopped following God's will), this cycle became just a meaningless and frustrating round of growth and decay. Romans 8 tells us that the whole of creation is longing for the day when we all start following the will of God again.

Plants and animals weren't eternal before Adam's sin— otherwise there wouldn't be any coal from dead forests or fossils from dead animals, and the planet would have been quickly overpopulated with animals that were reproducing and living forever. Animals experienced a lifecycle of birth, reproduction, and death. But Adam was special: God picked him out because he wanted the company of him and his descendants for eternity. When Adam and Eve failed their test, they were forced to rejoin the rest of creation and follow the cycle of birth, reproduction, and death again. But they didn't go back to being mere animals—they were irrevocably different because God had given them a spirit, making them into human beings.

The tree of life reappears in the human story at the very end of the Bible. The intervening chapters describe how God wonderfully provided restoration to everlasting life for the descendants of those first two human beings. Now he lovingly invites everyone to live in the new world he has created for those who accept his remedy for their sin. The whole new earth will enjoy the perfection of Eden because the tree of life will no longer be confined to a single garden: a large number of these trees will be planted as an avenue in the eternal city (Rom 8:21; Rev 22:2). Perhaps this is what God planned from the start—that the garden of Eden would have grown into a garden city where billions of people could live safely, while still being able to explore the natural planet around them.[7] In that case, his plan wasn't frustrated by sin—it was merely postponed.

---

7. See chap. 14, "Ecology and the New Earth."

SUMMARY

- Adam's life-giving tree can be regarded as a source of regenerative food supplement.

- The other tree could have been God's early warning of rebellion in the new, morally free humans.

- Death started in humans due to their exclusion from the source of life extension.

- *Proposal:* Outside Eden the natural cycles of death occurred, but this became a meaningless frustration when humans stopped following God's will for the planet.

19

▾

When and Where Did Adam Live?

Paleoanthropologists trace humans back three million years, so where does Adam fit in? Details in the text of Genesis reveal some intriguing possibilities that correspond with what archaeologists and geneticists have discovered.

I t's easy to interpret the account of Adam and Eve as a representative story or a foundation myth.[1] These are plausible interpretations that I wouldn't rule out, but I believe it is worth seeing how far we can get by assuming that the narrative describes actual events. The language used in Genesis has been constrained by the limitations of ancient vocabulary, and the account omits a lot of details that we, but not the author, are interested in. However, this doesn't mean that we can't think about how it might fit in with what we have found in nature. As careful readers of early Genesis, we are left with a whole range of questions about Adam and Eve: Why did God make human beings? Where was Eden? How did God make Adam? What was Eve made from? and When did it all happen? Let's see how the narrative might fit in with what we have found in nature.

---

1. Unlike most chapters, this one and the next frequently refer back to previous chapters in its section, so you'll have an easier time if you read them first.

The only one of these questions that Genesis is concerned to answer is *why* God created human beings. The implied answer is that he wanted to have a relationship with us—as illustrated by the way he went for a stroll in Eden to talk with Adam (Gen 3:8). Of course, this leads to all kinds of supplementary questions such as why God would give us freedom, knowing the inevitable trouble that he would have to sort out. After all, he is complete in himself and doesn't need us. Genesis doesn't answer that question, but perhaps those of us who are parents know that the frustration—and even pain—that comes hand in hand with having children is more than worth it.

With regard to the remaining questions, we have to turn to various other sources of knowledge to find possible answers because the Bible isn't concerned with these topics and provides very scant information.

WHERE WAS EDEN?

Since we are attempting to interpret the Bible as a straight-forward narrative, asking where Eden was should be treated as a worthwhile question. And Genesis encourages us to ask it because it names four nearby rivers (Gen 2:10-14). Geographers can only identify the Tigris and Euphrates for certain: they both start in eastern Turkey and end in southern Iraq. No one has yet found a perfect garden in either location, but what should we expect if its gardeners were expelled?

Throughout the centuries, the inhabitants of the area bounded by the southern end of the Tigris and Euphrates would have said that their land was the original Eden: it was full of waterways, copious wildlife, and a great variety of plants. But in the 1990s the occupants rebelled against Saddam Hussein, and in revenge he drained their land by diverting rivers. The soil was quickly ruined by a buildup of salt, which killed the vegetation and wildlife. However, the Eden Again project has started to reverse this ecological disaster.[2]

A better guess for Eden's location is the northern origin of these two rivers, near the Karacadag Mountains, where agriculture was invented about 10,500 years ago. (This also happens to be near Göbekli Tepe—a sophisticated religious monument five thousand years older than the pyramids or Stonehenge.[3]) Agriculture started with a mutation in a species of grass that prevented its seed falling to the ground when it matured. Normally a plant with this mutation would have died out, because if the seed stays on the plant, it can't germinate in the ground. But someone realized they would no longer have to pick up individual mature seeds off the soil if they grew this variety. Instead, they could reap the plants and thresh them to make the grains fall off in a heap, then plant a few to grow the next crop. This was a wonderful convergence of human intelligence and an otherwise useless mutation. Every grain of wheat now grown in the world can be traced to this mutation, which occurred about 8000 BC on that mountainside at the northern origin of the Tigris and Euphrates—that is, at the location that the Bible describes for Eden. Is this a coincidence?

WHAT WERE ADAM AND EVE MADE FROM?

Genesis is clear that God made human beings into something different from animals. After making Adam from dust, God breathed into him, and this is presumably when Adam gained a spirit, unlike all other animals, which merely have a soul

---

2. See Iraq Foundation, "Draft Report Physical Characteristics of Mesopotamian Marshlands of Southern Iraq," January 2003 (TinyURL.com/EdenAgainIraq).

3. See Asle Rønning, "On the Track of the World's First Farmer," Science Nordic, January 31, 2012 (TinyURL.com/FirstFarmer).

(Gen 2:7).[4] The spirit that God put inside Adam wasn't the Holy Spirit, but our human spirit, and it transformed Adam from what we might call a "human animal" into what we can call a "human being."[5]

Adam was made from dust (Gen 2:7).[6] This sounds special, but the Bible later describes God making all of us the same way: "you molded me like clay"; "all [people] come from dust" (Job 10:9; Eccl 3:20). Since we are all made of "dust"—that is, of matter—like Adam, when Genesis uses that same phrase to describe the way that Adam was made, this may imply that he was made like us, by means of parents.

Eve was made in a completely different way from Adam— we read that God used a "rib" from Adam (Gen 2:21–23). Three verses describe this—almost as much as each "day" in Genesis 1—so this was clearly a significant event. The Hebrew *tsela* usually means "side" but can mean "rib," and that makes sense in this context. Our lowest ribs are floating—that is, they don't reach to the sternum at the front—and removing one would have no consequences. Actually, a small portion of humans have an extra, thirteenth rib, and if Adam had this, it certainly wouldn't have been missed.[7]

As usual, the text doesn't tell us about the process itself, because teaching *how* things were done wasn't its objective. It just says, "God caused the man to fall into a deep sleep; and while he was sleeping, he took one of the man's ribs and then closed

---

4. See chap. 16, "Animals Have Souls in the Bible," and chap. 17, "What Does the Human Spirit Do?"

5. See chap. 18, "Adam's Apple in Literal Language."

6. See chap. 15, "Made from Dust, Like Adam."

7. See J. F. G. M. Costa, J. Brito, A. Costa, F. Caseiro-Alves, and A. Bernardes, "Normal Variants in the Chest: Mimickers of Disease," European Society of Radiology (TinyURL.com/RibChanges).

up the place with flesh," then he "made a woman from the rib ... and he brought her to the man." The first part sounds rather like an operation—a rib being extracted under anesthetic. The next part sounds like cloning. Of course, it could not have been straightforward cloning, because that would result in a male. In order to make a female, the Y chromosome had to be discarded and the X chromosome doubled. Also, when we make a clone today, we induce a cell to become an egg, which divides into a blastocyst and then forms a fetus. If God followed this process when he made Eve, Adam would have had to sleep for several years while she grew to adulthood. This was possible, of course—though presumably God could have used faster cloning techniques.

But why was Eve made this way? Why didn't God simply use the same method he had used to create Adam? The different way in which God formed her is an important clue about what made Adam special. Presumably, whatever this special thing was, it had to be passed on to Eve because, as Adam said, she was "bone of my bones and flesh of my flesh." If the account was written today, Adam would no doubt say, "She shares my DNA"—and it would seem that this is what was special about Adam. God had developed an individual with the exact DNA that he wanted, and then he made a feminized clone from Adam's genes to make sure that the traits he wanted were passed on.

Perhaps these specific genetic traits included the ability to interact with a spirit. In an earlier chapter,[8] I compared the brain to a computer and the human spirit to a router that can access the spiritual "internet." In this analogy, I said that the brain needed facilities akin to a keyboard by which it could interact with this spirit. In animals that lack a spirit, such as an ape,

---

8. See chap. 17, "What Does the Human Spirit Do?"

which is very similar to a human, there is no need for this "keyboard" facility. This is the facility that Adam had and none of the nonhuman animals had: it enabled his brain to interact with the spirit that God gave him. In other words, Adam would have been that individual who finally, after billions of years of development, had the specific brain adaptation necessary to interact with God on a spiritual level.

Genesis presents Adam as the conclusion and reason for God creating the universe—to make someone who could share his love. So God put him somewhere he could be safe, with a tree to feed him supplements that enabled him to live forever.[9] And then God set about replicating Adam's DNA, first by making a feminized clone and then by letting them reproduce sexually—the method built into creation. Their offspring would inherit this same ability to interact with their human spirit.

WHEN DID ADAM AND EVE LIVE?

Bible chronology isn't straightforward, because the Hebrew for "father" and the verb "to father" can also mean "to be a grandfather" or "ancestor" (e.g., 2 Sam 9:7, where the same word means both "father" and "grandfather"). So although Genesis 5 lists Noah's nine most famous ancestors, we have no idea how many generations came between each of them. If you read this as if it were written in English—that is, that they all simply "fathered" the next person—Adam would have been born about 4000 BC. In the seventeenth century, Bishop James Ussher calculated his birth date as 4004 BC, and this was repeated so often in the margins of printed Bibles that it became accepted as fact. The Bible text itself, however, doesn't give us specific dating.

---

9. See chap. 18, "Adam's Apple in Literal Language."

In order to pinpoint the time, we need to identify something that might be preserved in the archaeological or genetic record that indicates when human animals become human beings. The traits we might expect a spirit to give humans, such as concepts of prayer, worship, empathy, and cooperation, aren't things that can be seen by an archaeologist or geneticist—until those humans build something such as an altar. So perhaps this change will coincide with something else that we can detect. If it occurred first in just one or two people, we are not looking for something that transformed the whole human population at once; we are searching for a change that gradually spread through its offspring and conferred enough advantage to cause everyone who lacked this ability to gradually die out.

Perhaps this change is indicated by the capability of human speech. This ability is due to a small genetic change that slowly spread throughout the population. It conferred a significant advantage so that all living humans today share it, which means that all those without it have died out. This change took place in the gene FOXP2 sometime before five hundred thousand years ago. Geneticists discovered its importance when investigating a few individuals with mutations in this gene, which caused a severe speech impediment and an inability to understand grammar. It also has several other functions, including lengthening brain dendrites to enable faster learning.[10]

Although this is a promising theory, things are never quite so simple. This change in FOXP2 occurred before the first exodus from Africa of individuals who became Neanderthals and Denisovans in Europe and Asia, respectively, while the ancestors of modern humans stayed in Africa for thousands of years before

---

10. See Wikipedia, "FOXP2" (TinyURL.com/WikiFOXP2).

they followed them.[11] This means that these other groups who preceded modern humans also had the ability to speak.[12] So speech itself does not mark the change conferred to Adam.

The so-called mitochondrial Eve and Y-chromosome Adam both lived about 150,000 years ago,[13] so could they be the Bible's Adam and Eve? These titles are rather misleading because they don't refer to a single person from whom all humans descended but merely the person from whom the DNA of all *living* people descended, without taking into account the DNA of families that have died out.[14] If the flood was global, the Y-chromosome Adam would be Noah, because this method only looks for a common genetic ancestor and not for the true ancestor of all the people.

Perhaps a better indicator for the change from human animals to human beings is the sudden increase in brain size that came with the human version of gene MCPH1, which arrived about forty thousand years ago. The role of this gene is clear when it goes wrong and causes the terrible condition of microcephaly.[15] This isn't the only gene that determines intelligence, but it looks like this one sets humans apart. This human version of gene MCPH1 arrived at the same time that Cro-Magnons (another name for modern humans) left Africa and started spreading through Asia and Europe.[16] They met Neanderthals

11. See "The Age of Homo Sapiens," Atlas of Human Evolution (TinyURL. com/HumanSpread).

12. See Philip Lieberman, "Language Did Not Spring Forth 100,000 Years Ago," PLoS Biology 13 (February 2015) (TinyURL.com/NonHumanSpeech). On Denisovans, see Wikipedia, "Denisovan" (TinyURL.com/WikiDenisovans).

13. See Ewen Callaway, "Genetic Adam and Eve Did Not Live Too Far Apart in Time," *Nature*, August 6, 2013 (TinyURL.com/AdamEveGenetic).

14. See Wikipedia, "Mitochondrial Eve" (TinyURL.com/EveMito).

15. See Wikipedia, "Microcephalin" (TinyURL.com/Microcephalin).

16. See K. Kris Hurst, "Why Don't We Call Them Cro-Magnon Anymore?," ThoughtCo, January 17, 2018, (TinyURL.com/NotCroMagnon).

and Denisovans along the way, and sometimes interbred, but these prehuman groups soon died out.

We have found the first musical instruments—hollow bones with holes, like a flute—from about this same time, alongside which archaeologists found the earliest "Venus figurine," small figures usually shaped as pregnant or recently pregnant females.[17] Personalized burials also started at this time, with grave goods, which may have been believed to help the deceased in the afterlife.[18]

Some of these advances have been previously linked with Neanderthals, as well as with the modern humans that succeeded them. One early study found evidence of Neanderthals putting flowers in one grave, though this is now widely discounted, and claims about Neanderthal art are also uncertain.[19] They certainly buried their dead sometimes, but this may merely have been to stop the corpses smelling and attracting wild animals to their area. It seems, therefore, that the more spiritual aspects of life, such as concerns about the afterlife, music, and art, were specifically linked with humans from about forty thousand years ago.

At about twenty thousand years ago, there was another less dramatic but perhaps more significant revolution—in cave

17. See "Earliest Musical Instruments Date Back 42000 Years," Sci News, May 25, 2012 (TinyURL.com/FirstMusic); Wikipedia, "Venus of Hohle Fels" (TinyURL.com/VenusHF).

18. See Wikipedia "Burial" (TinyURL.com/WikiBurial).

19. See Wikipedia, "Shanidar Cave" (TinyURL.com/ShanidarCave); Jeffrey D. Sommer, "The Shanidar IV 'Flower Burial': A Re-evaluation of Neanderthal Burial Ritual," Cambridge Archaeological Journal 9 (1999): 127–29 (TinyURL.com/NeanderthalBurial); Robert Gargett, "Grave Shortcomings: The Evidence for Neandertal Burial," Current Anthropology 30, no. 2 (April 1989) (TinyURL.com/GargettGrave); Maxine Aubert, Adam Brumm, and Jillian Huntley, "Early Dates for 'Neanderthal Cave Art' May Be Wrong," Journal of Human Evolution 125 (2018): 215–17 (TinyURL.com/NeanderthalArt).

paintings. Before then, art all over the world, from France to Borneo, consisted of pictures of animals. After this date, artists all over the world started including images of humans in their pictures—but the reason for this change is unknown.[20] I sometimes wonder how we would know if an AI has become conscious, and I think that we would suspect this if it attempted a self-portrait. In the same way, something occurred about twenty thousand years ago that suddenly made humans look not only at those things outside their group but also at themselves. They became literally self-conscious.

This simplified summary of the many stages in humanity's complex history shows how difficult it is to pinpoint the time when God breathed his spirit into that single man. The new insights and abilities that this brought would have been likely to spread quickly throughout the population (as we'll explore in the next chapter). Adam's descendants were a completely new type of human that we have called "human beings" (because no other term currently exists) to distinguish them from "human animals" (who no longer exist). As well as having a spirit that enabled them to be aware of God, they could empathize with each other more deeply. This would make cooperation better and communities more successful. Colonies of these new human beings were also united by their newfound spiritual insights, which gave them a purpose and a reason to work with each other even if this meant personal sacrifice.

Spotting this change in the records of archaeology or genetics may not be possible, especially as Genesis does not tell us what to look for. The best guess we have come up with is the

---

20. See Brian Handwerk, "World's Oldest-Known Figurative Paintings Discovered in Borneo Cave," Smithsonian, November 7, 2018 (TinyURL.com/OldestPaintings).

development of artistry about forty thousand years ago, or self-conscious art about twenty thousand years ago. Even if Genesis intended to state the specific change that occurred, Moses and his contemporaries didn't have the language for concepts such as genetic inheritance, development of species, or millions of years. Nevertheless, Genesis does succeed in teaching the essential truths: that God was in charge and that he did all this so that we can come to know him. God is concerned that we should at least know what the original plan was, and also the happy ending: that he didn't abandon the human race when Adam failed.

SUMMARY

- Eden may be near the origin of wheat in the Karacadag Mountains and the oldest temple in Göbekli Tepe.

- Eve could be a feminized clone from Adam's DNA.

- They had the FOXP2 and MCPH1 genes for language and the extra ability to communicate spiritually.

- *Proposal:* Adam may have lived twenty thousand years ago, when humans started displaying self-conscious artistry.

20

▼

Where Did Cain's Wife Come From?

If Cain married someone living outside Eden, this would explain some strange details in Genesis. It would also explain how our gene pool contains so much variation.

I'm one of those annoying people who rarely get sick. It isn't that I live a charmed life and avoid infections—I had all the normal childhood illnesses of measles, chicken pox, and mumps, but none of them caused me much suffering. I even caught tuberculosis (which can kill you) and mononucleosis (which can lay you out for months), but I didn't have any treatment because I didn't feel ill—I only knew I'd had them when they showed up in medical tests later. I recently found the likely cause of my good health when I had my genes mapped: I've inherited lots of Neanderthal DNA, which includes a heightened immune system.[1]

This chapter will *not* conclude that Cain married a Neanderthal—though I love the idea that his punishment included marrying someone stronger who could stand up to him. However,

---

1. See Helen Briggs, "Neanderthal Genes 'Boosted Our Immunity,'" BBC News, January 7, 2016 (TinyURL.com/Neanderthal-Immunity).

our genetic inheritance is much richer and more complex than we'd expect if we had all descended from one incestuous family. As we'll see, it is nonetheless possible that we all descended from Adam and Eve and still gained a rich gene pool.

Cain could, of course, have married his sister—though the Bible doesn't say this happened. It is difficult to imagine her wanting to marry a brother (especially the nasty brother who murdered the nice one). Presumably this incest wouldn't be dangerous like it is today because God could have made sure there weren't any dangerous recessive genes in Adam's chromosomes. However, our human race would be very weak if the entire gene pool had been limited to just Adam's chromosomes. Restricted gene pools often cause problems in overrefined agricultural animals or crop lines because this makes them vulnerable to pests and changes in the environment. This is solved by interbreeding with wild species to reinvigorate the gene pool by introducing more variety.

DIVERSE GENE POOL

Fortunately, the human gene pool does have a lot of healthy variety. This includes far more than just differences in skin color and facial features; the most important differences are invisible, such as our biochemistry and immune system. A lot of this variety has no actual benefits at present, but variety future-proofs the species. Without it, we might get wiped out by a new type of infection that attacks a process that is identical in all of us. Our gene pool is very robust because the genes in our human population have a wide range of varieties (technically known as alleles).

For example, we have three major blood types, A, B, and O, which all work well. These are produced by three significantly different versions of a single gene called ABO. Mixing blood of type A with type B will cause agglutination, which will kill someone who gets the wrong transfusion, but mixing with O is unproblematic. We all have two copies of every gene, so someone with A+A or A+O is blood type A; B+B or B+O is type B; and A+B is type AB. The rare person with O+O is particularly useful because they can be a donor for anyone.

Actually, the situation is much more complex: there aren't only three versions of this gene—there are about seventy.[2] These seventy versions of the ABO gene divide into these three major groups, so normally we can ignore this complexity. But how did we get seventy different versions of the same gene if our ancestors are only Adam and Eve? They could only pass on four different versions of the ABO gene at the most. And if Eve was a feminized clone of Adam (as the text seems to imply), then there were only two versions of that gene available.

It is possible, of course, that in the meantime mutations would produce more versions of the gene, but that would require a much faster rate of mutation than we see at present—in fact, it would be dangerously fast. Other genes have vastly more varieties—such as MHC (Major Histocompatibility Complex), which has eight hundred different forms.[3] The mutation rate would need to be extremely high to produce all these differences in just a few thousand years.

Mutations occur very rarely, unless there are carcinogens present. This is good, because most mutations are dangerous—as seen by the effects of carcinogens. Reproductive cells are protected from mutations by DNA repair mechanisms, which make sure that accidental mutations are rarely passed on to our

---

2. See Wikipedia, "ABO Blood Group System" (TinyURL.com/ABO-BloodGroups).

3. See Wikipedia, "Gene Polymorphism" (TinyURL.com/WikiPolymorph).

children. A few do get through—on average sixty-four mutations—though this is tiny compared to the three billion base
pairs that are copied perfectly.[4] However, some of these are so
harmful that they result in miscarriage—about 10 percent of
pregnancies end this way. So even a small increase in mutation
rate would result in a *lot* more miscarriages.

The low mutation rate means that a new variety of a gene
takes a long time to develop. The multitude of ABO varieties
would take millions of years to arise—longer than humans have
been around—so it's not surprising to find that most are already
present in other primates, from whom we presumably inherited
them.[5] These different varieties don't confer any advantage, so
there would be zero chance of them having occurred in humans
by parallel evolution. This ABO gene is just one of the twenty
thousand genes in our chromosomes, most of which also have
several different versions that could not have been inherited
from only two individuals.

Very occasionally, a mutation gets inherited that makes a
really useful difference. The FOXP2 gene has two tiny differences
that produced the most significant development between us and
chimps: language. Chimps have a slightly better version than
the one in mice, whose FOXP2 gene only enables them to make
ultrasonic squeaks—a single change enables chimps to make
more complex noises. These kinds of useful changes happen
only once in thousands or millions of years because inherited
mutations are rare, and useful ones are extremely rare. They
are rare because the mutation rate is low, and this has to be low
because most mutations are dangerous.

---

4. See Wikipedia, "Mutation Rate" (TinyURL.com/WikiMutationRate).

5. See Laure Ségurel, "The ABO Blood Group Is a Trans-Species Polymorphism in Primates," *Proceedings of the National Academy of Sciences of the USA* 109
(November 6, 2012): 18493–98 (TinyURL.com/ABO-Primates).

Of course, God could at any time force an advantageous change to occur, so that useful evolution speeds up. However, the timescale over which changes have been observed to happen suggests that our genetic inheritance has been allowed to progress naturally. God could have interfered, but it appears that he was happy to let his creation work in the way he had designed it.

NEANDERTHAL DNA

If all human beings did descend from Adam, we have to account for the diversity that now exists in our genome. This includes not only the large number of variants among human genes, but also the genes from prehumans—including Neanderthals and Denisovans—which many of us have. The most likely source of all these different genes is something the Bible doesn't mention (but also doesn't rule out): that there were human animals living at the same time as Adam.

As I mention in chapter 19, when using the term "human animal," I mean humans that were like Adam before God put a spirit into him. The Bible implies that the presence of a spirit that can communicate with God is what makes humans different from animals.[6] If God made Adam from the dust, like he makes us from dust,[7] then God picked him from a group of animals that looked exactly like him. They remained animals, while God made Adam into a "human being"—with a spirit that was passed to all his descendants. God put Adam into Eden, while the other human animals continued to live outside the protective wall around this special garden. This means they couldn't eat from the tree of life that would have enabled Adam to live forever.

---

6. See also chap. 17, "What Does the Human Spirit Do?"
7. See chap. 15, "Made from Dust, like Adam."

When Adam's family were thrown out of Eden, they would have been able to mix with these human animals and breed with them—though they probably wouldn't want to. We don't know whether their children would inherit a spirit like God gave to Adam, but there is a good reason to think that they would: a spirit was not withheld from Cain. Even after Cain had murdered his brother, we know he had a spirit because he was able to hear God ask him, "Where is your brother Abel?" (Gen 4:9). Adam's two sons, Abel and Cain, were very different. Abel is called "righteous" (Matt 23:35; Heb 11:4), but Cain clearly wasn't. And yet both of them inherited a human spirit. This suggests that God's gift of a spirit to Adam's family was irrevocable, and that every child inherited one and retained it whether they acted morally or not. In that case, if Cain married a wife who was a human animal (i.e., a human without a spirit), why would God stop Cain's descendants from inheriting the human spirit?

This is pure speculation because the Bible doesn't tell us whom Cain married. We can't be sure that he married someone outside Eden, because the Bible doesn't mention the existence of humans who hadn't received a spirit like Adam did. But neither does the Bible rule this out—it is simply silent about it. We are equally unsure that Cain married a sister, because the Bible is silent about that too. All the text tells us is that he got married and went to a land called "Nod," where he founded a city (Gen 4:16–17).

Actually, if Cain did marry someone outside Eden, this helps to explain quite a few interesting details in the text—for example, his fear that "whoever finds me will kill me" (Gen 4:14). Of course, he could simply be inventing some danger, so that his family wouldn't make him leave. However, God took him seriously and said that "anyone who kills Cain will suffer vengeance seven times over," and he "put a mark on Cain so that no one who found him would kill him" (v. 15). Who was Cain afraid of, if Adam's family were the only humans on earth? At the time, Adam had no son other than Cain. So even if he was afraid that a future son of Adam would come after him for revenge, Cain would have a twenty-year head start to get away out of danger. However, his fear that he would meet someone "out there" makes perfect sense if human animals lived outside Eden.

Although I use the rather derogatory term "human animals," there is no reason to think that they were less intelligent than the human beings—Adam and his descendants. They had the genetic capability to speak and think as intelligently as human beings (i.e., those with a spirit). They presumably showed the full range of human emotions, just like other intelligent animals. What they lacked was the ability or desire to communicate with God. If a colony of them had survived in a hidden spot on the planet, we would have found people who had no religion. That doesn't mean they would be like atheists, because they wouldn't feel any need to deny God's existence either—the idea of God would never arise. We would expect them to display no appreciation of religion or any interest in pursuing the topic when it was introduced, and they probably wouldn't think of doubting it any more than they doubt that the North Pole exists. We have never found a tribe like that, but it isn't impossible.

LIFE OUTSIDE EDEN

If other human animals did exist at the time of Adam, this helps to explain other curious matters we discover in the text of Genesis. One of these is obvious but not trivial: Where did Cain find a wife? The text simply says: "Cain went out ... and lived in the land of Nod, east of Eden. Cain made love to his wife" (Gen 4:16–17).

This sounds strange—the wife seems to appear out of nowhere. He either took a sister with him, or there was already a colony of human animals east of Eden and Cain married one of them.

The description of Cain's life also makes more sense if there were already others outside Eden, because it explains who lived in the "city" (or "town") that he built. Genesis says his wife "became pregnant and gave birth to Enoch. Cain was then building a city, and he named it after his son Enoch" (Gen 4:17). We could, of course, interpret the text as, "She gave birth to Enoch. Cain was then [much later] building a city [to house all his grandchildren and great-grandchildren]." Or instead, it could describe Cain wanting to organize the people among whom he lived, and starting by founding a town where they could live closer together.

Human beings (those descended from Adam) may have been much better at cooperating and organizing people than human animals because they had the empathy to understand the motivations and feelings of others. It is therefore not surprising that Cain would be the one to start bringing them together. Building towns was a key step in the progress of the human race because it enabled individuals to specialize in different roles. An isolated family needed to know how to build a house, breed crops and animals, and invent and create tools, then spend time teaching all this to their children. People in a town could specialize as builders, farmers, inventers, artisans, and teachers.

So we aren't surprised when Genesis says about Cain's descendants that "Jabal ... was the father of those who live in tents and raise livestock. ... Jubal ... was the father of all who play stringed instruments and pipes. ... Tubal-Cain ... forged all kinds of tools out of bronze and iron" (Gen 4:20–22). In fact, we would expect Cain's children to fare much better than the children of others because his family carried the inheritance from

God: a spirit that raised them above the human animals. Even if they didn't use their new insights to search for and to follow God, their spirit still gave them other advantages.

It is difficult to imagine what a human would be like without a spirit because presumably they have all died out by now, just as the Neanderthals and Denisovans died out thirty-five thousand years ago. A spirit would give human beings many minor advantages and two major ones. First, they would be aware of God and be able to call on him for help and guidance. Second, they would be much better at cooperating with their fellows. This was really important in times of famine or other problems when only those who stuck together would survive. And sometimes a colony would only survive because individuals were willing to sacrifice themselves for the sake of unrelated fellow humans. This is something you are much more willing to do if you believe that fellow humans are all children of God and that there is life after death—concepts that are related to possessing a spirit.

NO CONFLICT

The suggestion that many human animals lived at the time of Adam might seem shocking at first, but it is important to realize that this is not contrary to the text of Genesis—it is only contrary to our traditional interpretation of it. In fact, it makes better sense of some aspects of the text, especially with regard to Cain. Breeding with this other type of human sounds wrong at first—although perhaps not as wrong as marrying a sister. And breeding with these outsiders conferred the advantage of a wider gene pool, something that is now important to us.

Cain didn't marry a Neanderthal, because they are likely to have been long extinct. However, some humans had bred with them, so their genes were mixed into the human race. If Cain and his descendants married human animals outside Eden, their children would gain a double advantage—of being spiritual (through Cain and Adam's side of the family) and of having a superb immune system from the side whose ancestors had bred with Neanderthals.

The wide variety that consequently exists in the human gene pool means that we have been able to adapt to almost every environment on earth—from the unending heat of the tropics to the barren cold of the poles and the oxygen-depleted heights of the Andes. Our children can be very different: athletic, nerdy, exploring, nurturing, combative, or caring. Not only has this diversity enabled me to inherit unusual health, but it has given the whole of humanity a healthy gene pool which helps us to survive. This was surely part of God's plan when he made us as part of his creation. He arranged for us to inherit benefits from all of our ancestors, not just from Adam. However, Adam has given us all a most important legacy: our spirit that can communicate with God, and (unfortunately) our sinful rebelliousness.

SUMMARY

- Humans benefit from a wide gene pool with much more variety than one recent couple could supply.

- The Bible does not rule out "human animals" that lived without the spirit that was in the "human beings" descended from Adam.

- These human animals would be less capable of empathy and cooperative, so their descendants were less likely to survive.

- *Proposal:* Cain and others widened the gene pool by breeding with humans outside Eden, and all descendants of Adam were born with a spirit.

Section 4

▾

Humanity

21

▾

What Is Male and Female?

A surprising proportion of babies are born physically intersex—that is, not identifiably male or female. The Bible only condemns those who live contrary to their nature, which implies that God accepts us as we are—however we are born.

She was a shy twelve-year-old, like me. When she kissed me before jumping on a bus, I fell in love a little—in a hopelessly confused way. We were both much more confused a week later when she reported what hospital tests had revealed. She had been diagnosed with a severe intersex state: she had both ovaries and internal testes—that is, "she" was both male and female.

When I looked into the issue, I was surprised to learn that more than one in two thousand babies need a specialist to determine their gender, and surgery was often used to "normalize" them soon after birth.[1] Increasingly, surgery is discouraged at a young age, so that the child can have a chance to establish their gender identity later in life. Others, like my friend, have intersex problems that only reveal themselves at puberty. Understandably, very few of those with these conditions talk about it, so the difficulties they face remain largely hidden.

---

1. See Intersex Society of North America (TinyURL.com/IntersexFeq).

GENDER IN THE BIBLE

The Bible has a curious double message on sexuality: it emphasizes the distinction between male and female but deemphasizes the differences. The Law of Moses outlawed a man wearing female clothing and vice versa (Deut 22:5). Since both sexes wore long robes, this wasn't for modesty reasons but to ensure that everyone knew your gender. However, the Israelites did not treat women as differently as we might expect. Women could work outside the home, for example, as a shepherd—like the women that Jacob and Moses married (Gen 29:9; Exod 2:16). They could also work on someone's farm or buy and sell things in a market (Ruth 2:8; Prov 31:16, 24). And although there were no female priests, the priests' wives ate temple food that was forbidden to nonpriests (Lev 22:13), so God himself didn't perceive them as less holy.

Genesis honors Eve very highly. In saying that Eve was made from Adam himself, Genesis emphasizes similarity rather than differences (Gen 2:21). The King James translation calls Eve a "help meet for him" (Gen 2:20). In older English, "meet" meant "fitting" or "suitable," but in modern English this makes her seem like a domestic servant. However, the words "meet for him" translate the Hebrew word *kenegdo*—a combined word meaning "like + beside + him"—that is, she is very similar to Adam and on a par with ("beside") him. The surprise lies in the word "help" (Hebrew *ezer*) because the Bible always uses this word for someone who is *more* powerful—it is often used to refer to a warrior who defends you, and usually it is used for God himself who helps you.[2] So in contrast to what we might assume, Eve was more like Lara Croft than a Stepford wife!

---

2. E.g., Ps 115:9–11; see STEP Bible data at TinyURL.com/EveHelper.

THE STRUGGLE TO FIT IN

But sexual identity isn't always straightforward. Not everyone is born a square-jawed, strong man or a full-lipped, curvy woman like those populating the beaches of *Baywatch*. Among all of us ordinary people are a surprising number whose gender is somewhere between male and female. The most serious and most common chromosome defect is Klinefelter's syndrome, where instead of having male XY chromosomes or female XX, a person has XXY. Hormonal problems such as congenital adrenal hyperplasia (CAH) result in male development in a fetus that has female chromosomes. There are about a dozen other different causes for a bewildering array of variations or mixtures of male and female features.[3]

It is very difficult for those who have these intersex syndromes to fit into a society where everyone is either male or female. It is arguably harder for those who have perfectly normal chromosomes but nevertheless have poorly or differently developed genitals or behaviors because they have nothing to point to as the cause—except that they are different. These situations often arise from a mixture of hormones in the womb between the eighth and twenty-fourth weeks of gestation, shortly before birth, or at puberty—the three critical stages of sexual development. These hormones can even come from outside the person—from the environment or the mother. Studies with rats have found that even short bursts of such hormones during critical stages of pregnancy can result in normal genitals but transgender behavior. In humans, 30 percent of female babies who

---

3. See Wikipedia, "Intersex" (TinyURL.com/WikiIntersex).

experienced high testosterone due to CAH grow up with homo-sexual inclinations.[4]

One biblical principle is that God loves us as we are. The demands of society may force us to conform in all kinds of ways—in clothing, manners, food, and sexual stereotypes—but we shouldn't blame God for this. Paul is sometimes regarded as being heavy-handed about conformity—for example, he didn't want Christians to unnecessarily offend anyone by eating the wrong food or wearing the wrong headwear (1 Cor 8:9-13; 11:13-16). In spite of this, when it came to conforming to expectations of sexuality, he recognized that people have different experiences of sexual desire. Paul himself preferred singleness and encouraged it, but he also accepted that marriage was good, and in fact preferable for those who might otherwise fall into sexual immorality (1 Cor 7:7-9). Paul summarizes the Christian attitude to these differences concerning sexual desire with this principle: "Let each person lead the life that the Lord has assigned to him, and to which God has called him" (1 Cor 7:17 ESV).

CONTRARY TO ONE'S "NATURE"

Paul also applies this principle when presenting some very forceful teaching against homosexual behavior. Instead of presenting a general criticism, he specifically pointed at those who *changed* to this from their former sexuality. He articulates this emphatically in Romans 1: "They *exchanged* the truth about God for a lie. ... Their women *exchanged* natural sexual relations for unnatural ones. In the same way the men also *abandoned* natural relations with women" (1:25-27, italics added). The words

---

4. See Melissa Hines, Mihaela Constantinescu, and Debra Spencer, "Early Androgen Exposure and Human Gender Development," *Biology of Sex Differences* 6 (2015) (TinyURL.com/IntersexHormones).

"exchanged" and "abandoned" imply that their original nature and lifestyle was heterosexual, but they deliberately took up homosexual behavior. He isn't referring to those who find that they can't respond to the opposite sex—that is, those who were born that way. Instead, he specifically refers to those who have "abandoned natural relations with women"—that is, they already had heterosexual relationships that were "normal" to them and then chose to pursue homosexual relationships.

Roman society was full of these practices that Paul was condemning, and he was pointing the finger at some very powerful people. Emperor Tiberius trained boys to arouse him underwater while he swam, and Nero married a male slave while dressed as a bride, consummating it publicly. There are similar records of homoerotic behavior by almost every early emperor, and such hedonistic homosexuality was rampant in Roman society. They were deliberately trying something different simply to stimulate their jaded sexual appetites, and Paul was rightly outraged by this kind of practice, which was contrary to nature—that is, to the way they were born.

Acting contrary to nature was at the heart of Paul's condemnation: "their women exchanged *natural* sexual relations for *unnatural* ones. In the same way, the men also abandoned *natural* relations with women" (Rom 1:26-27). The concept of "nature" (*phusis*) can refer to "natural law" (as in Rom 2:14), "created nature" (as in Rom 11:24), or "society norms" (as in 1 Cor 11:14). In Romans 1, we can rule out the last meaning because Paul would not tell us to conform with the norms of the very society that he was criticizing. So he must mean one or both of the first two.

If he means "natural law," then Paul is referring to something that everyone knows is wrong, because the law is written into nature itself. That is, he is saying that even Gentiles know this behavior is wrong, just like everyone knows that murder and theft are wrong. If he means "created nature," then Paul is referring to something that can be inferred from the nature of creation itself. That is, he is saying "you shouldn't act in a way that contradicts the way you were created." I think it is likely he means both, because this puts him in line with the principle of 1 Corinthians 7:17 that everyone should "lead the life that the Lord has assigned to him." In other words, by *natural* law everyone knows that they should not change the *nature* that God has given them.

THE WAY GOD MADE US

God loves us—whatever nature we have been born with. Those born with any of the varieties of intersex states can take comfort that the Bible doesn't demand we conform to society, but it asks us to accept the way that God has made us. Those with gender dysphoria may have been brought up as the "wrong" gender, because gender identity and body shape may misalign with each other while being formed in the womb. This can cause a lot of heartache and overt or silent criticism, but God loves us as we are—not as others think of us.

Paul specifically criticized those who change their sexuality—but doesn't criticize those who are rejected by society for being who they already are. The reason he gives for his criticism is that those who change their nature are rejecting the nature that God their creator gave them. By giving this as the reason, he isn't just being silent about those who are born that way—he is explaining why they are excluded from his criticism.

A few societies easily accept those who have varying degrees of intersex states. In India, *hijras* (who dress as women but have male features) are paid to bless marriages and births. In 2013,

India even introduced an intersex gender birth certificate.[5] Native North American *berdaches* dressed as men for warfare and as women at other times, and in several tribes they were considered to be powerful healers.[6] Even in Bible times, Assyrian culture had nonmale men known as *kulu'u* who were cultic actors.[7]

Western societies have only recently woken up to the complexities of human sexuality, and the Bible is usually blamed for this late willingness to engage with the issue. It is true that the Bible makes clear distinctions between male and female, especially with regard to dress, and those who were natural eunuchs or had other sexual ambiguities weren't allowed in the Temple (a rabbinic rule based on Deut 23:1). But when Jesus came, he showed that this didn't imply God was rejecting them because he said that some, such as himself, were willing to be like a eunuch for the sake of the kingdom (Matt 19:12).

The sciences have now taught us more about the true complexity of human nature, and we now recognize the varieties of personalities that God has created. It has been something of a revelation to look back at the Bible with these insights and see that it was not as binary with regard to sexuality as we had thought. It turns out that the Bible is more sympathetic than many societies are. This should come as no surprise, because God made us as we are and loves us all as we are. The challenges for us are to agree with him and to do the same.

---

5. See Supreme Court of India report "Writ Petition (Civil) No.400 of 2012" (TinyURL.com/IntersexBirthCert).

6. See "Berdache," Encyclopedia of the Great Plains (TinyURL.com/Berdaches).

7. See A. R. George, "Part Three: A Commentary on a Ritual of the Month Nisan," *Babylonian Texts from the Folios of Sidney Smith* (TinyURL.com/GeorgeKuluu).

SUMMARY

- One in two thousand babies are born with uncertainty about their physical gender, caused by hormones or genes.

- Paul teaches that God accepts us as we are. Paul condemns those who change their sexual behavior to something contrary to the nature they were born with.

- **Proposal:** God loves us as we are, so we shouldn't reject those who are different in various ways.

22

▾

Where Does Altruism Come From?

Acts of kindness and self-sacrificial heroism occur in all populations. Are they signs of divine action in someone's life, or are they simply normal traits that we should expect to find in humans?

When disasters such as fires, earthquakes, or tsunamis strike, we often see the best side of humanity. People rush in to rescue complete strangers, spending hours carefully clearing rubble to find victims or flying to dangerous situations just to help those who are suffering. They don't do this for fame or fortune, and their own families gain nothing. Sometimes groups are organized by churches and other religions, but the volunteers are just as likely to have no active faith or even be militant atheists. So what motivates us to do good?

The Bible can be interpreted as saying that humans are incapable of doing good without God's help and motivation, and that he gave us laws to make sure we recognize our sinfulness. Another interpretation is that we can do *some* good, and that God's laws are to encourage and educate us to do better, though this goodness is never enough to undo our sin. Which is right? Are we capable of doing good without God's help?

The Bible is realistic about humans right from the start; none of us have ever been faultless. Even when humans were in the perfect environment of Eden, without any provocation or needs, they had the inclination to break rules. We can recognize ourselves in the account of Adam and Eve; we, too, would end up ignoring the prohibition not to eat from the forbidden tree — either because we were curious or we wanted self-advancement, or simply because it was a challenge.

ALL HAVE SINNED

The rest of the Old Testament confirms that humans repeatedly ruin their lives and the lives of others by breaking moral codes and rules of law; and the New Testament presents the theological conclusion: "All have sinned and fall short of the glory of God," because we are "slaves to sin" who are merely "gratifying the cravings of our flesh" (Rom 3:23; 6:20; Eph 2:3).

Some theological systems take this further, almost to the point of saying that humans can't do anything that is really good. This is a common interpretation of the Calvinist doctrine of total depravity. Strictly speaking, though, Calvinism doesn't entail the idea that humans are incapable of doing good. This theology says only that they are incapable of deciding by themselves to repent of their wrongs and turn to God because every part of them, including their minds, is affected by sin.

The existence of altruistic and other "good" behavior toward strangers is sometimes used as proof that God's goodness affects humans, because a purely evolutionary approach would predict that you only help those who are genetically related to you.[1] This is confirmed somewhat by animal studies. For example, red

---

1. E.g., Brad Harrub, "Altruism and Evolution," *Apologetics Press: Reason & Revelation* (April 2005) (TinyURL.com/HarrubAltruism).

squirrels will sometimes adopt a baby squirrel if the mother has been killed by a predator, but researchers found they had to be somewhat related to the mother.[2] This is similar to the way that people are more likely to help each other if they can find some commonality—such as being from the same ethnic group or religion.

However, it is nevertheless true that most people will naturally help someone whether or not they are related. This suggests there is a biological basis for this apparent natural goodness.

HUMAN COOPERATION AND GOD'S LAW

Recently some interesting work in the field of anthropology has helped to explain how morality can naturally arise in a human population.[3] It suggests that the need for cooperation in times of food shortages means that individuals who are good at teamwork and collaboration with others are more likely to survive and have children than loners who try to find food on their own. Since we inherit a lot of characteristics, such as extroversion and introversion, we are also likely to inherit the tendency to cooperate. Therefore, most of us are descended from those who were good at cooperating with people who weren't necessarily part of their family, because they were the ones who survived disasters such as famines.

If someone loses the trust of others, perhaps by stealing more than their share from the food store, they will be expelled from their community, so they are less likely to have any descendants. However, if they then show contrition and convince the others

---

2. See Brian Murphy, "Red Squirrels: Altruists or Self-Serving Survivalists?," EurekAlert, June 2, 2010 (TinyURL.com/AltruisticSquirrels).

3. A good review of the following ideas is in Jonathan Birch, "Book Review: Michael Tomasello // A Natural History of Human Morality," *British Journal for the Philosophy of Science* (2017) (TinyURL.com/TomaselloMorality).

that they won't do it again, they may be readmitted and survive. So another characteristic we are likely to inherit is a sense of guilt and the wish to be reconciled with people we have hurt. This is a possible start to what we might now regard as a moral code, along with concepts of remorse and restitution.

This theory makes sense as an origin for human morality and the capability and desire to do good deeds toward others. In early history, humans needed to work with each other in order to successfully hunt wild animals such as aurochs—an ancestor of the cow that was as large and agile as a horse but as dangerous as a rhinoceros.[4] If we are descended from people who successfully worked in teams, this could explain why it seems more exciting to achieve something alongside others rather than just by ourselves. It's true that we get a sense of gratification from completing something on our own, but that is very different from the high-fives and whoops of mutual congratulation that greet the completion of a difficult task by a team. That most of us prefer to work in groups and get lonely on our own might suggest that we are mainly descended from those who *did* cooperate rather than from the loners, whose family line tended to die out in famines.

If our morals do spring from our need to cooperate, we'd expect them to be universal—the need for moralists to teach them to "uncivilized" societies would simply not exist. Indeed, Christians who have tried to convert Native Americans and Māoris found that they already knew that theft, adultery, and greed were wrong. In fact, the "natives" were also sometimes surprisingly altruistic—willing to share their meager food with missionaries who had come unprepared—though, of course, many

---

4. See Wikipedia, "Aurochs" (TinyURL.com/WikiAurochs).

others were not so welcoming. These missionaries had to learn that preaching the gospel was not about civilizing and teaching morality, but teaching about Jesus, who had a cure for sin.

But if human goodness can arise simply by a history of cooperation, what part does God's law and his guidance play in our lives?

I think it is significant that the first home given to humans in the Bible was a garden, in which the first pair were told to cooperate by tending it together. Subsequently, God gave the Israelites laws forbidding murder, theft, or even coveting what belongs to your neighbor. These laws also encouraged cooperation because you are much more likely to trust someone if they don't lie or steal from you. Jesus later internalized these laws by turning them into attitudes. Instead of outlawing murder and theft, Jesus said we should not hate or retaliate when wronged, and we should show love even to our enemies (Exod 20; Matt 5). Jesus therefore turned laws into a morality that helps to hold society together.

Paul said that the purpose of the law was not only to inform us what is right and wrong, but also to tell us that we are bad and not righteous (Rom 3:19-20). But it also had another purpose: to help us improve and become a better person than when we started. We inherit a sinful nature that tempts us to commit acts such as adultery, lying, or stealing for our own benefit, but God wants to help us overcome that tendency and to grow in virtue. The Old Testament was only able to list the offenses that God wanted us to try to avoid, but the New Testament tells of a new power that will help us succeed—the indwelling Holy Spirit. The process of sanctification—making us as holy as the Holy Spirit within us—becomes the goal and purpose of life for someone deciding to follow Jesus.

NATURAL GOODNESS

If our tendency to cooperate and help others is inherited, then some people have a head start on being "good." Some individuals are born with naturally "good" characteristics, in that they are innately empathic and willing to work together with and help others. Other individuals are born with unhelpful or difficult characteristics such as selfishly caring only for their own needs and wants. Although they accept the help of others, they rarely reciprocate unless they think they will gain by doing so.

A few individuals are born with "bad" characteristics that lead to antisocial behavior. This might range from committing acts of theft and damage, without any regard for the harm they cause, to deliberate cruelty in order to feel superior to others. Not many are born like this because, in the past, the family line of such individuals tended to die out. Being born with these "bad" traits doesn't excuse anyone for immoral behavior, but we should be aware that some people find it harder than others to be "good."

Whatever characteristics we are born with, we can change for the better. Those with bad traits can overcome them, and those who naturally do beneficial things can become even better. This is the process of sanctification for a Christian.

Theologically speaking, all types of people are sinners, whether they are naturally cooperative or naturally selfish, because no one is perfect. The Bible presents the apparently harsh conclusion that everyone is destined for hell, whether they are good or bad, unless they repent and turn to follow God. This seems unfair until we take on board the conclusion from social anthropology that we have inherited a lot of our morality. If God judged us by how much good or evil we did, some of us would be disadvantaged because we were born with a stronger inclination to be selfish, violent, or sexually promiscuous. The

Bible implies that God is not interested in our natural goodness or badness, but he is only interested in our repentance and willingness to let his Holy Spirit transform us.

This process of sanctification can transform us into someone more Christlike, but it won't have the same end result for everyone in this lifetime because we don't all start from the same point. Someone with a psychopathic personality who takes up charity work has clearly had his life totally transformed. If that same level of change were applied to the respectable people he works with who were born naturally empathetic and "nice," they would be transformed into absolute saints. In other words, you can't tell from the outside who has allowed themselves to be transformed the most.

None of us are born "good" in God's eyes, but as a society we regard some people as better than others. God sees the potential in us all and gives us a target to aim for. The direction and distance that we travel in God's strength is much more important than what we actually achieve in this life because in the end, when Christ appears, all those who follow Jesus will become like him (1 John 3:2). In the meantime, we each need to strive to let the Holy Spirit transform us into better people than when we first started. And, importantly, we need to do that without judging those who have had a greater handicap in that goal.

SUMMARY

- Atheists also volunteer to help when disaster strikes, so goodness in humans isn't always divinely empowered.

- Anthropological studies suggest morality and self-lessness are traits that would naturally arise due to the survival value of cooperative behavior.

- We can inherit a propensity to these good characteristics and also to bad character traits such as violence and selfishness.

- *Proposal:* Sanctification of a believer involves the Holy Spirit making us more Christlike, but some have a head start, so we should not look down on those who have traveled along a harder and steeper road.

23

▼

Can God Become a Real Human?

Jesus was fully man, with a limited human mind, so how could he know everything that God knows? One solution lies in analogies with computers and especially within some popular computer games.

When my young daughters discovered the life-simulation computer game *The Sims*, they became creators of their own universe. They could "make" virtual people, giving them the physical features and personality characteristics that they determined— cheerful, creative, romantic, self-assured, and so on. And they could then prompt their virtual creations to do things such as cleaning the toilet (otherwise it became infested with flies) or applying for a job. If their Sim wasn't knowledge-able or creative enough to perform their job well, their charac-teristics could be adjusted. You could make them practice so that they gradually improved, or you could employ a cheat code to immediately download extra skills into them.

This type of game is the modern equivalent of the ant farm that I remember building as a child. You half fill a thin glass or plastic container with sandy soil, and put sticks and leaves on top. Then you introduce a colony of ants and watch them dig out tunnels and make a home. You can choose to help the ants by supplying more leaves and other food, or you can disrupt their plans by pushing a twig into the soil to cut off some of their tunnels.

Thinking about these computer characters and ants is a good starting point for us to try to imagine how Jesus felt about becoming a human. In Philippians we read that Jesus humbled himself, leaving behind his greatness, glory, and power, and that he became as lowly as a slave (Phil 2:6–8). But this is only half the story. Because the human brain is limited, Jesus also had to leave behind most of his knowledge. He could no longer be omniscient—knowing everything in the universe—because there is only so much room inside the human skull. So how did Jesus cope with the limitations of our human brain? And could he still be regarded as being God if he could only remember as much as we can?

A SERIOUS DOWNGRADE

Perhaps we can begin to have an idea of what it was like for Jesus if we try to imagine becoming an ant—a serious downgrade, to say the least. Our brain has about 100,000,000,000 nerve cells, but an ant brain has only 250,000. We would also lose most of our independence because we'd do things only in response to the aims of the colony. Our communication would be limited; instead of having about a million words of English at our disposal, we could only pass signals using a few chemicals. And our job satisfaction would be reduced to carrying things, such as pieces of dismembered enemies or half-chewed leaves.

Children soak up information, but as we get older, we have to forget things in order to make room for new knowledge. Mostly we do this by simplifying what we know—discarding most of the details of an event and remembering only the smell or the emotion associated with it, or perhaps a single image. But eventually the whole event is lost, and the engram (a unit of memory) is reused for something completely different.

Was Jesus ever actually ignorant of something? One possible example was when he said this about the coming destruction: "that day or hour no one knows, not even the angels in heaven, nor the Son, but only the Father" (Matt 24:36 = Mark 13:32). It isn't surprising that some early Christians tried to deny this. Some scribes went as far as leaving out the words "even the Son" from these verses, so that it was only people and angels who were ignorant.[1] Others said that Jesus wasn't limited by having a merely human mind, but he actually retained his divinely omniscient mind within a human body. Irenaeus vehemently denied this revision as a heresy because he said that Jesus had to be fully human in his mind, as in every other part of his humanity, in order to save us. He said that salvation involved Jesus becoming like us, and if he became only partly like us he would only partly save us.[2]

SUPERNATURAL KNOWLEDGE

And yet, Jesus also had supernatural knowledge at times. When some Pharisees thought that he had blasphemed, "Jesus knew in his spirit that this was what they were thinking in their hearts" (Mark 2:8 = Luke 5:22), and similarly he knew the thoughts of other people (Luke 6:8; 9:47). John said that Jesus didn't entrust himself to certain people because "he knew what was in each person" (John 2:25), and he records that Nathanael's doubts disappeared when Jesus told him "I saw you while you were still under the fig tree before Philip called you" (John 1:48). Luke

---

1. See the data from STEPBible.org at TinyURL.com/STEP-Ignorant.
2. See Irenaeus, *Against Heresies* 2.28.6 (TinyURL.com/IrenaeusHumanMind).

records a story from Jesus' childhood that implies he already understood more than the teachers in the Temple (Luke 2:46–47).

If Jesus had a normal human mind, how did he also have this supernatural knowledge? It might be that, in these instances, he was using a "word of knowledge," whereby the Holy Spirit told him what he needed to know (as in 1 Cor 12:8). However, the way Mark describes it, Jesus knew these things in his *own* "spirit" (Mark 2:8), and the other texts simply state that Jesus knew these things.

So we are left with something of a dilemma. As Jesus' human mind could not hold all of his divine knowledge, and a human mind cannot read the minds of others, the implication is that he had special powers and wasn't really a normal human. But this is precisely the heresy that Irenaeus was so concerned about.

One solution is that the knowledge that Jesus needed was communicated directly to his spirit by his Father. Something like this happens in computer games or the *Matrix* movies when a character needs extra skills (such as how to fly a helicopter): that knowledge is downloaded straight into their brains. Although that character's brain can only hold a limited amount of information, they can potentially know anything that is stored on a server, ready for download.

READY FOR DOWNLOAD

Similarly, as Jesus' spirit was in constant communication with his Father, anything that his Father knew could be communicated to him. It was as though he had an instant-access connection to the largest information server in the universe, so whatever he needed to know could be downloaded as required.

This doesn't mean that Jesus was superhuman, because he wasn't doing anything that wasn't possible for a believer or a prophet who was listening to God. The unique thing about Jesus was his sinlessness and holiness, by which he was able to remain so close to his Father that he could receive such knowledge easily. This meant he could even claim, "I do nothing on my own but speak just what the Father has taught me" (John 8:28).

Considering theological questions about the incarnation in the light of computer technology raises some intriguing possibilities for ourselves, as well as Jesus. For instance, as one day we will be "like Jesus" (1 John 3:2), we too may have access to this knowledge, at least in part. I love being able to look things up quickly on the internet, and I can only imagine what it would be like to download anything from the omniscient mind of God into my own mind whenever I need it.

SUMMARY

- God's reduction to human limitations was greater than us becoming an ant with four hundred thousand times less memory.

- Jesus' limited human brain couldn't know everything, and yet he knew what people were thinking.

- In fiction and computer games, we are familiar with the idea that knowledge can be downloaded into someone's mind.

- *Proposal:* Jesus was able to download knowledge from his Father as needed because he was so close to him.

24

▾

The World Is Improving— Statistically

Statisticians say the world is getting better in most ways, but doesn't the Bible predict the opposite? Jesus said that when disasters happen, the end is "not yet," and Paul expected Jesus' return when everyone says, "Peace, peace."

When Christians hear about disasters and violent events, they often act strangely: with sadness at the suffering accompanied by a kind of smug "I told you so" look, saying, "Well, the Bible predicted this would happen." But is this really what the Bible says? If so, we have a problem, because the facts suggest that collectively we are actually suffering less than in previous generations.

We are bombarded with news. Thirty-minute TV news shows have been supplemented by twenty-four-hour channels, and newspapers now compete with hundreds of reputable internet sites—as well as millions of disreputable sources. Bad news from across the world is widely reported, while good news is rarely reported, because experience has shown that good news just isn't as interesting. The few "positive" or "encouraging" news items are saved for a happy end to the news program. Today we know much more about disasters, wars, and crimes than we would have years ago, so it's understandable that we might conclude that the world is getting worse. But how true is this?

CRIME AND WAR

Let's look at crime statistics. They consistently show that fewer reported crimes have occurred in almost every category since the 1990s.[1] However, these figures appear misleading because the news is still full of crime stories. In the UK these numbers are collected in two ways: by counting crimes reported to the police (recorded crimes), and by asking thirty-five thousand households each year whether they have suffered any crime (the crime survey). The crime survey confirms the UK has followed the US's downward trend in personal experience of crime, but there has been an *increase* in recorded crimes. It appears that people are now more likely to report a theft or a fight outside a pub that, in the past, wouldn't have involved the police.[2] As a result, surveys of how people *feel* about crime indicate the perception that crimes are steadily increasing.

And what about wars? Estimated death figures show that an average of 260,000 people per year were killed in the Thirty Years' War of 1618–48, and 300,000 per year died in the Napoleonic Wars of 1803–15.[3] In the two World Wars, 3.7 million and 14.1 million respectively were killed per year.[4] The numbers certainly

---

1. See US figures at Nathan James, "Recent Violent Crime Trends in the United States," Congressional Research Service, June 20, 2018 (TinyURL.com/CrimeUSA), and UK figures in "UK Crime Trends Not So Clear Cut," Knoema, October 30, 2017 (TinyURL.com/CrimeFigsUK).

2. See Rachel Schraer, "Crime Figures: Is Violence Rising?," BBC News, January 24, 2019, (TinyURL.com/ViolenceMoreOrLess).

3. See Wikipedia, "Thirty Years' War" (TinyURL.com/30YWar); "Napoleonic Wars" (TinyURL.com/WikiNapoleon).

4. Based on World War I deaths of sixteen million over 4.3 years, and World War II deaths of seventy million over 5.4 years—though more people died from

appear to be getting dramatically worse. However, when we take into account population increases over those periods, we find that the proportion of people killed did not increase so dramatically: the wars killed 0.056 percent, 0.03 percent, 0.18 percent, and 0.3 percent of the world population, respectively.[5] These figures still show an increase, but the earlier wars involved a much smaller area of the world. If we compare wars in the same specific area, we see that the fatalities actually fall with time, despite the increasing power of weaponry. For example, the Thirty Years' War wiped out a third of the German population, whereas 6.4 percent of the population were killed in World War II, including civilians.[6] Since World War II there hasn't been a single year without devastating wars, including thirteen with more than a million casualties, and yet the total number of people killed per year keeps falling dramatically.[7]

All this warfare is horrifying, but the likelihood of an individual being killed in one is constantly falling. We now realize that every life matters, and we no longer regard the lives of soldiers, let alone civilians, as expendable. So our perception of human suffering due to war continues to increase.

---

nonmilitary actions. See Wikipedia, "World War I casualties" (TinyURL.com/CasualtiesWW1) and "World War II casualties" (TinyURL.com/CasualtiesWW2).

  5. Based on world populations of 0.5 billion in 1600, 1 billion in 1800, 2 billion in 1927, and 2.5 billion in 1945. See Wikipedia, "World Population" (TinyURL.com/WikiWorldPop).

  6. Based on 4.5 million dead and a postwar population of 65.3 million. For various totals see Wikipedia, "German Casualties in World War II" (TinyURL.com/WW2German).

  7. See Piero Scaruffi, "Wars and Casualties of the 20th and 21st Centuries" (TinyURL.com/ScaruffiCasualties).

PERSECUTION AND FAMINE

Religious persecution, by contrast, escalated dramatically since 2011 because of attempts by organizations such as ISIS and Boko Haram to establish Islamic rule. They and others worldwide have killed tens of thousands of Christians and a much larger number of different types of Muslims. Their death toll is on a par with the Roman emperor Diocletian in the early fourth century when he attempted to wipe out Christianity. According to ancient reports, seventeen thousand Christians died in a single month and twenty thousand died in a single city (Nicomedia, in Turkey). Although these numbers are comparable with the murders of Christians by ISIS, the number of Christians alive in Diocletian's day totaled perhaps only a million compared with the two billion today—so the proportion martyred today is comparatively tiny. An individual Christian was in far more peril in that terrible past than they are today.

This rise in the level of people killed by terrorism can be exaggerated in our perception by constant media reports. Steven Pinker, who should be credited for pointing out our modern misconceptions about increasing violence, has shown that this recent increase in terrorism is minor blip.[8] Oxfam conducted a sobering comparison of annual fatalities from different causes. They use an average baseline of 13,000 deaths from terrorism; instead, let's take a baseline from the worst year ever: 44,000 deaths in 2014. Compared to this, an average person is 27 times more likely to die in a traffic accident, 64 times more likely to die as a result of obesity, and 136 times more likely to die from smoking.[9] These common causes of death don't make exciting

8. See Stephen Pinker, "Has the Decline of Violence Reversed since *The Better Angels of Our Nature* Was Written?" (TinyURL.com/PinkerStats).

9. See "What If We Allocated Aid $ Based on How Much Damage Something Does, and Whether We Know How to Fix It?," Oxfam Blogs, March 7, 2013

news stories, so the number of reports about terrorist deaths gives us a wrong perception about their number.

Plagues and famines have also filled our news recently with terrifying details. Ebola has killed about 11.5 thousand individuals,[10] the AIDS epidemic has so far claimed 36 million deaths worldwide, and Covid-19 may end up killing 0.5 percent of the world's population.[11] But proportionally this is far less than the Black Death, which killed 60 percent of Europe's population in the fourteenth century,[12] or the diseases brought to the Americas, which killed more than 90 percent of the native population. The worst recent pandemic was the flu of 1918, which killed about 70 million people—4 percent of humanity.[13] There has been nothing that horrific recently.

Even famines don't kill like they used to, thanks to world food aid. There have been significant decreases in rainfall, especially in the US and northern Africa, so the causes of famine are still with us, but now we cope better with them. Of course, there are exceptions caused by war or in areas permanently altered by climate change, but thankfully even these don't cause famines on the scale of those in the past. There is still terrible suffering due to food shortages in some areas, but there are now four times as many people who are overweight than underweight.[14]

(TinyURL.com/AidPolicy).

10. See Wikipedia, "West African Ebola Virus Epidemic" (TinyURL.com/EbolaW-Africa).

11. I write this in spring 2020 during the middle of the outbreak, when total deaths have reached 200,000, so the actual outcome may measure how pessimistic or optimistic I am.

12. See Ole Benedictow, "The Black Death: The Greatest Catastrophe Ever," *History Today* 55, no. 3 (March 2005) (TinyURL.com/BlackDeathCatastrophe).

13. See "Outbreak: 10 of the Worst Pandemics in History," MPH Online (TinyURL.com/WorstPandemics).

14. See "Double Burden of Malnutrition," World Health Organization (TinyURL.com/DoubleBurden).

Of course, statistics don't tell the terrible stories of individual suffering. That an individual is less likely to suffer from persecutions, war, famine, and disease does not lessen in any way the horror of these events or our need to respond with help and compassion for those enduring them. Nevertheless, we must be careful not to play false with reality.

THE END IS NOT YET

But didn't Jesus predict that things must get worse and worse until he comes? Actually, Jesus described only one sign that indicated his coming was imminent, and listed several others that he said did *not* portend the end: "You will hear of wars and rumors of wars, but see to it that you are not alarmed. *Such things must happen, but the end is still to come.* Nation will rise against nation, and kingdom against kingdom. There will be famines and earthquakes in various places. *All these are the beginning* of birth pains" (Matt 24:6–8, italics added).

Among all the signs that Jesus listed, only one indicated that the end is near: "this gospel of the kingdom will be preached in the whole world as a testimony to all nations, *and then the end will come*" (Matt 24:14). In other words, don't be worried when these other things happen—they will certainly come about, but they do not indicate that this is the end. Paul agreed; he expected Jesus to come after a period of quiet, when everyone will be saying "Peace, peace" (1 Thess 5:3).

Predicting the end of the world has been the pastime of many Bible interpreters since the time of Jesus. There was a great increase of interest near the year 1000, and then again when the fire of London occurred in such a seemingly significant year— 1666! Perhaps one day there will be a terrible war in the Middle East that is interrupted by Jesus' coming, or perhaps the world will get gradually better until we welcome his coming—the Bible isn't clear, and I don't see much point in trying to guess before-hand because that isn't the purpose of Bible prophecy.

The reason Jesus warned us about wars, famines, and per-secutions was so that when those terrible things happened we would know that God hadn't lost control. The ancient and medi-eval church suffered much more than we do from the actions of both non-Christians and (tragically) from different types of Christians. It took comfort from the fact that Jesus had pre-dicted these things. But Jesus didn't say they would continually get worse, and he specifically didn't link them to his coming. Yes, there is still terrible suffering in the world today, but we can't be sure whether it will increase or decrease before the end, because Jesus didn't tell us.

TEST YOURSELF

Statistics that have been collected with scientific rigor are often ignored even by educated thinkers and influential leaders. Hans Rosling was a medical statistician who regularly surveyed his audiences before he spoke. At the 2015 World Economic Forum in Davos, he asked world leaders about their perceptions of the world they helped govern before presenting them with the facts. Here is part of his survey for you to try yourself:

- In the last twenty years, the proportion of the world living in extreme poverty has: (a) almost doubled, (b) remained more or less the same, (c) almost halved.

- How did the number of deaths per year from nat-ural disasters change over the last hundred years? (a) more than doubled, (b) remained about the same, (c) decreased to less than half.

- How many of the world's one-year-old children today have been vaccinated against some disease? (a) 20 percent, (b) 50 percent, (c) 80 percent.

After reading this chapter you probably guessed that all three answers are (c). If you got it wrong, you can comfort yourself with this: the one thousand world leaders at Davos did worse than they would have if they picked answers at random.[15] Statistics like these don't just educate us about the world we live in; they also tell us a lot about ourselves.

Our reaction to bad news is what causes our faulty perception. Our nature is to worry and to expect the worst because we remember bad things more clearly and longer than good things. In some ways this is a healthy response—like pain is—because it helps to make us aware of danger and thereby prevents us from getting hurt. But, like pain, it can also ruin our lives. Our natural levels of optimism or pessimism also color our reaction. After all, optimists think we are living in the best of all possible worlds, while pessimists fear this is so.

Paul had a remedy for this tension: "Finally, brothers and sisters, whatever is true, whatever is noble, whatever is right, whatever is pure, whatever is lovely, whatever is admirable—if anything is excellent or praiseworthy—think about such things" (Phil 4:8). Our grandparents' generation concluded from this that we should count our blessings and give thanks. In the secular world this was encapsulated as "the power of positive thinking." New studies in happiness conclude much the same: that the happiest people are those who are mindful of the good things in

---

15. See Hans Rosling, *Factfulness: Ten Reasons We're Wrong About the World—and Why Things Are Better Than You Think* (New York: Flatiron Books, 2018). A fuller test is at TinyURL.com/FactfulnessTest and a good review at TinyURL.com/FactfulnessReview.

life and specifically the good things that happen to them.[16] So the route to contentment recommended by Paul and our grandparents really works—whether or not the world is getting worse.

SUMMARY

- Constant news reports give the impression the world is becoming more dangerous on average.

- Statistics show that an individual is becoming less likely to be harmed by natural or man-made disasters.

- Jesus predicted disasters but didn't say things would be worse at the end.

- *Proposal:* The world is gradually improving as the gospel spreads to the whole world. Jesus said he would return when this goal was accomplished.

---

16. See James Clear, "The Science of Positive Thinking: How Positive Thoughts Build Your Skills, Boost Your Health, and Improve Your Work" Huff-Post Life blog, July 10, 2013 (TinyURL.com/HuffpostPositive).

25

▾

Human Resurrection by Backup?

Computer science presents us with a vocabulary for understanding resurrection: our DNA and body can be reconstructed like hardware, and our memory can be backed up like software. Of course, the backup drive would be huge.

Memory is largely an illusion—that's the sad conclusion of neurologists. We remember only a fraction of what happens to us, and then we fill in the gaps. Our brains simply don't have the capacity to retain everything. And we forget things, because the brain cells that hold old memories are gradually reused for new ones. It poses a rather interesting question for Christians: Can we expect to get all our memories back when we are resurrected? Analogies drawn from computer backup technologies can put new realism into this Christian hope. As for the hardware—the resurrection of our bodies is also now easier to comprehend thanks to developments in genetics.

We can now envisage God recreating our bodies to be the same as the ones we inhabited, because we are familiar with concepts such as cloning. Former generations thought that God would reconstruct our bodies from our bones. This belief was based partly on the fact that bones can last almost indefinitely if they are kept dry, and partly on the amazing vision in Ezekiel 37, where God raised up a valley of dry bones as living people. This is why Christians and Jews buried their loved ones, and first-century Jews even scraped remaining flesh off the bones of their dead after a year, then transferred them to a clean, dry ossuary, which successfully preserved them to this day. Christians and Jews regarded cremation (which was practiced by Greeks and Romans) as irreligious, and it has only gained acceptance in Christian countries during the last century.

A NEW BODY

Paul said that the new resurrection body will be very different from our old one—as different as a plant is from a gnarly seed, or the sun is from the moon (1 Cor 15:37–41). Jesus said that these bodies won't have any reproductive functions (Matt 22:30), presumably because they won't die—so having offspring won't be necessary. And if Jesus' resurrection body is any guide, they may also be able to travel by novel means, such as through locked doors (John 20:19, 26). So these will be utterly new bodies and not just animated corpses. It doesn't matter whether the atoms used by our original body have been eaten by a worm, then fed to a fish, which was then eaten by a person. God can still raise everyone to life using atoms from elsewhere by basing it on the pattern that our body had.

God could use our genome to reconstruct a virtually identical body. A body with identical DNA may not be exactly identical, because identical twins are genetic clones and yet they often look subtly different. The Bible implies that God will do more than just create a clone, because Jesus' resurrection body bore records of his life history—in particular, the scars of his death, which are a permanent part of his glory. Our resurrection body may also include features from our life history that make us recognizable, such as laugh lines and perhaps even pregnancy stretch marks, though presumably we won't have any painful disabilities.

One of Jesus' parables implied that we will recognize our friends (Luke 16:9), though I'm hoping that my college friends will recognize me more easily than recent friends—it would be nice to look a few decades younger! Interestingly, when Jesus' friends and disciples saw his resurrected body, they didn't immediately recognize him (John 20:14–16; Luke 24:16). This may be a confirmation that God does indeed use our DNA to create our resurrection body so that it may be subtly different and perhaps younger than the body that died.

WHAT ABOUT JESUS?

This brings up a difficult and potentially divisive theological question: Was Jesus' resurrection special, or was it the same that his followers will experience? We might initially think that because Jesus is special in all kinds of ways, his death and resurrection was different. His followers won't go to hell before being raised (like he did—Acts 2:31; 1 Pet 3:19), and unless they die just before his return they will be dead for much longer than a couple of days. Jesus was alive again before his body had suffered much decay, so we usually assume that his resurrection body was simply his reanimated corpse. Until recent centuries, most Christians assumed that they, too, would be raised from their buried remains, so Jesus' resurrection didn't seem significantly different. But if everyone else receives a brand-new resurrection body, while Jesus' new body was his reanimated corpse, then his resurrection was different and (arguably) inferior to ours.

There is also a theological problem: if Jesus' resurrection was different, then can he really be the "firstborn from among the dead" (Col 1:18; Rev 1:5)? That is, Jesus was born and lived in a fully human way in order to represent us completely when bearing our sin; he suffered real human death just like us, so that when he rose from that death he was opening the door for us to rise in the same way (Rom 5:17; 1 Cor 15:47–49). He was like us "in every way" (Heb 2:17), so we might expect his resurrection to be like ours too. In other words, after he died, we'd expect his Father to give him a brand-new body so that those who follow him will be like him (1 John 3:2).

When theologian David Jenkins was asked this question in 1984, he said he believed that Jesus' new body was not his old corpse, and he was castigated for not believing in the "real" resurrection of Jesus. "If Jesus was given a new body," people asked, "what happened to his original body which disappeared from the tomb?" Unfortunately David answered this with a memorable but provocative phrase: "The resurrection was not just a conjuring trick with bones." A former college friend of his told me that this was typical of the kinds of jocular phrases he liked to use— but this time, no one laughed. He was not a student now—he was about to become the bishop of Durham. Journalists picked up this phrase and twisted it, saying that he had compared the resurrection to a conjuring trick with bones. And when lightning caused a fire in York Minster a few days after he was consecrated bishop there, it seemed as though God agreed with his critics.

PROOF OF CONCEPT

So how can Jesus have a new resurrection body when his old body was apparently reused? This question is worth thinking about even if we can't come to any definite conclusion. After all, if resurrection bodies can be constructed from different atoms based on the recorded pattern of DNA plus any significant personal features, then the actual corpse isn't needed. In Jesus' case, however, there was no need to collect some atoms that might be available to build his resurrection body. The most obvious available source was his newly killed corpse. Just as a brand-new picture can be painted on a previously used canvas, a new body can be constructed from the atoms of an old one. So God could create a brand-new resurrection body, with all its improved features, out of the materials of Jesus' old body.

The resurrection of Jesus was, as engineers would call it, a proof of concept. Every new product needs a prototype, and every new process needs testing—and it worked. Jesus was alive again. Of course, God had no doubt that it would work, but the physical and demonstrable resurrection of Jesus was important for humans to see and report to each other: it really happened.

Actually, making the body may be the easier part of the problem. We almost have the technology to do this already—as Dolly the sheep showed—though, of course, normal clones don't have the superior features of resurrection bodies.[1] The harder bit is preserving and transferring the memories and personality.

Making a new body with a perfect skeleton instead of arthritic joints is pointless if the brain is blank, but our brains aren't so easy to reconstruct. When we get a new laptop, we transfer all our backups (which we hopefully remembered to make), but how does that work with our memories? We are still trying to fathom how memory is encoded in the brain, but one thing is certain: our brains can't hold everything we have ever seen and read and heard—we have a finite space within our cranium.

Neuroscientists in one study discovered a "Jennifer Aniston brain cell" (named after the actress made famous in the comedy series *Friends*).[2] During direct neuron stimulation in preparation for brain surgery, they found a single cell that responded whenever a person saw her picture or her name, but that cell

1. See Hebrew University of Jerusalem, "Embryo Stem Cells Created from Skin Cells," ScienceDaily, May 2, 2019 (TinyURL.com/StemCellsSkin).

2. See Anna Gosline, "Why Your Brain Has a Jennifer Aniston Cell," *New Scientist*, June 22, 2005 (TinyURL.com/SpecificBrainCells).

didn't fire up for any other images or names. This suggests that a specific neuron in our brains can be devoted to coordinating a particular concept or memory. What happens to that memory if the cell dies, or if it is reallocated to another memory? I'm sure that remembrances of my wife occupy considerably more than one cell in my brain, but we know that Alzheimer's disease can turn these cells into useless amyloid plaques that remember nothing. Are memories lost forever if they disappear from the cells that store them?

TOTAL RECALL?

How much of our life on earth will we remember in eternity? Will every mealtime conversation be as clear as when you first heard it? Will you recall every raised eyebrow and expression on your friend's face as they spoke? What about the background music or the flavor of the food? And what about the details you didn't consciously notice, such as the face of someone on the edge of your vision or a word spoken while you were thinking about something else? We can't recall this level of detail even immediately after a meal, unless we record everything we see, feel, and experience. However, the memory in our recorder would run out of space in a short while, and even our capacious brains can't contain that amount of detail.

Our brains cope by editing out extraneous details. During sleep we move some medium-term memories into long-term memory, and we discard others. But nothing is permanent. Our brain has a limited number of memory engrams, and although our brains are huge, they are not infinite; so new memories supplant old ones that we haven't used for a long time. On the whole, we don't miss the bits we forget because we are great at filling in the gaps. We remember things that we think about regularly and forget the things we don't think about—so we usually don't notice they are gone.

Will those gaps in our memories be restored in heaven? The storage system needed to record the totality of all our memories would be truly massive. Perhaps it could be recorded "in the clouds" of heaven. When we refer to computer cloud storage space, we mean a computer server somewhere on earth—perhaps a basement in Seattle—but the cloud storage space of heaven can be as endless as the Large Magellanic star cloud, which contains ten billion solar systems. Considering the size of creation, there is a great deal of matter that God could use for memory storage—though, of course, he is likely to have a completely different kind of information storage system of his own that may not require any matter.

Even now, some people wear life recorders that capture a picture every few seconds along with continuous audio and transmit it to storage by Wi-Fi. I wore video glasses during a holiday in Rome, and reviewing it later I realized how many details I had forgotten. My wife, looking over my shoulder, wanted to know why I was looking at the backside of the woman walking in front of me. I said it was a narrow street, and I had to look somewhere—but she had a point.

This type of situation could become even more pressing in heaven if every memory is resurrected. Jesus has already warned us about this issue: "There is nothing hidden that will not be disclosed" (Luke 8:17). Paul gave us some minor comfort, though, when he said that unworthy sections of our life will be burned up at judgment (1 Cor 3:12–15). I like to think of this like edited segments of film being thrown on a fire so no one will ever view them. Part of our salvation and forgiveness means that all those sections of our lives when we weren't living for Jesus will be erased and forgotten. However, this means that some of us won't have many memories worthy of taking into heaven.

FULLY KNOWN

The Bible does suggest that we will have infinite knowledge in heaven because Paul said, "I will know fully, even as I am fully known" (1 Cor 13:12). This amazing statement implies that we will know everything as well as God does. It is difficult to imagine even a resurrection body that can contain all the knowledge that the infinite God possesses. We have no idea what kinds of bodies we will have, but whatever they are made of, we can't have an infinite mind like God himself has.

Here, too, modern technology enables us at least to imagine what the Bible is describing. Today we no longer need laptops with huge hard drives—we just need a fast connection to the internet. When we need something that isn't on our drive, it is downloaded, and anything that we add is uploaded, ready for when we need it. Similarly, our resurrection bodies may not need to contain much more memory than we have now, because when we need knowledge we will be in communication with our Creator, who knows everything.

The most detailed vision of our future existence at the end of the Bible also sounds like science fiction: we will live in a cube-shaped city made of transparent materials (Rev 21:9–23). The gold of the city will be so transparently thin that no lights are needed, because the light of God can shine through the whole city (vv. 21, 23). I wonder whether this could have been God's way of telling first-century readers about the total transparency of mind-to-mind communication? If this were the case, we won't just be in constant touch with God but also with each other, so there will be literally no walls to hide behind. At present I don't like that idea of total openness, but perhaps it won't be so bad in that new world when I won't have so many vices to be ashamed of.

No doubt the reality of the resurrection will be totally different than anything we can yet imagine. But the point of this chapter is that computer science has at least enabled us to *make sense* of Bible passages that previously seemed impossible, even though we cannot yet fully understand them. We now have a better insight into the wonders that God has prepared for us. Our memories in heaven can be limitless, and all the bad bits will be edited out. Everything that is lovely and done in God's company will be remembered, with all the sin and tears wiped out forever. The pains and evil that we experienced while holding onto Jesus will be recorded as victory rather than suffering, and the sins that Jesus has forgiven won't be recorded at all. This isn't just rosy editing; it is a new reality, bought for us by Jesus' death and proved to be possible by his resurrection.

SUMMARY

- A twin with identical DNA may not look exactly the same, and the resurrected Jesus wasn't recognized immediately.

- Jesus had scars to indicate his history, so a new body may have features that reflect our lives—such as laugh lines.

- Even a new body won't have infinite memory.

- **Proposal:** We may have access to our resurrected memory, which we can download when required.

Section 5

▾

Miracles

26

▾

Miracles That Employ Nature

God doesn't materialize things like a fictional wizard might. He tends to enhance or speed up nature when working miracles, as if he likes using the natural world that he has created.

I don't know about you, but I've noticed something odd about miracles in the Bible. I suppose all miracles might be said to be odd, so perhaps the word I'm looking for is *different*. In contrast to wonders performed by fictional genies or wizards, the biblical miracles are just ... more ... *natural*.

Take, for example, when one of Elisha's disciples was using a borrowed axe and the head flew off and landed in a deep river (see 2 Kgs 6:5–6). A genie or a wizard might have retrieved it by snapping their fingers so that it flew out of the water and landed on the riverbank or perhaps materialized on the end of the axe handle. God's method was to tell Elisha to chop down a branch from a tree, then find out from his disciple where in the river the ax-head had fallen in and throw the branch in at that exact place. When Elisha did that, the ax-head floated up to the surface, balancing on the branch, and they were able to lean over and pick it up.

When I read this, I ask myself: Why did Elisha have to cut a branch instead of throwing in something that was already available, such as a pebble or a twig? The answer is, presumably, that an ax-head can float on a large piece of wood naturally. But why did he need to lean over and pick it up? Presumably, it's because ax-heads don't naturally jump off logs onto a riverbank. And why did he need to inquire where the ax-head had fallen in? Perhaps it was to give him a better chance of thrusting the branch into the river in exactly the right place. Of course, even when he knew roughly where it was, it is still an impossibly small likelihood that the branch would hit the ax-head exactly the right way so that it flipped onto the branch then balanced there while they floated to the surface naturally. In fact, it is certainly miraculous. But this miracle involves nothing that actually goes against nature.

MORE FROM LITTLE

Even the biblical miracles that are impossible naturally are less contrary to nature than we might expect. For example, a genie granting the wish of a woman who was starving and had lots of debts would snap those clever fingers again, and dishes of food and bags full of money would materialize in front of her. However, when Elisha met a starving widow, he asked her what assets she had—only a small drop of oil left in her jar. He then told her to borrow as many empty jars as she could from friends and neighbors and to pour oil from her jar into them. Miraculously, the oil kept flowing into the other jars until the last was filled—and then it stopped. The widow sold the oil to pay her debts, with enough left over to live on (2 Kgs 4:1–7).

Again, this miracle leaves me asking questions. Why did Elisha need to ask the widow what assets she had? Presumably, it was because he didn't know supernaturally. Why did she have to go and borrow jars? Presumably, it was to save doing an extra miracle to create new ones. And why didn't Elisha just give the widow miraculous money instead of having her sell the miraculous oil? Perhaps it was because creating oil helped the whole community, whereas generating more money would simply devalue all the existing money (something governments should know by now). Or maybe it was because God is in the business of making natural things such as food rather than manufactured things such as coins.

This miracle of multiplying had a deliberate limitation: after the last jar was filled, the oil stopped pouring out. A similar limitation happened when Elijah fed the widow at Zarephath: the food stopped being replenished when the drought ended (1 Kgs 17:9-16). Similarly, the manna and quail that God provided the Israelites was temporary (Exod 16). And I assume that when Jesus fed the thousands with bread and fish, the food stopped multiplying at some point; otherwise no one would ever have baked bread or gone fishing again. This suggests that God restricts miracles to fulfill a need.

Another interesting point in all these cases is that the meals were multiplied out of food that already existed. Fictional genies or fairy godmothers traditionally materialize things from nothing or from something quite disparate—like Cinderella's coach from a pumpkin. But God produced oil from oil, quail from flocks of quail, bread from bread, and fish from fish.

This kind of consistency in Bible miracles in different books—which were recorded by believers separated from each other by different centuries and cultures—is pretty impressive. None of them describe miracles of materialization or limitless growth. Skeptics might think this shows that God can't actually do big miracles, but it would be hard for them to argue that these accounts were merely made up, because made-up miracles would be so much bigger and better.

USING CREATION

Let's take the text seriously and ask what it is teaching us. Why do most miracles in the Bible occur in this natural and somewhat limited way? Perhaps it's because it's better for us that way. After all, powerful miracles could be dangerous. If you wanted to get rid of an annoying fly in the room, you could chase after it and swipe at it with a heavy shoe until you eventually squashed it, but you may well end up smashing up the room in the process. On the other hand, you could open all the windows and doors and wave something at it to help it find its way out. It may be that using more natural mechanisms (such as encouraging the fly to exit through the window) is less dangerous to the delicate mechanism of nature.

Or perhaps God simply prefers to do miracles this way. After all, he created nature, so he probably likes to use his creation. We often do the same: artisans like to use tools they have made themselves, programmers like to use their own algorithms, and teachers like to use their own lesson plans. God made wood that floats and iron that sinks, and so he enjoys using those qualities. He made food to grow for us, so he multiplies oil and fish, but not money or oil jars. God isn't limited, but he does have his favorite methods.

His main method for getting his will done is to use his creation—the plants, the soil, and especially his people. Usually he can rely on us to see what needs doing naturally. But when we can't see it (or when we don't want to see it), he gives us a prompt. If we are listening, he could prompt us by his Spirit. But even when prompting us, God tends to use the most "natural" means (i.e., he uses the creation he made) by getting other people to point out what needs to be done or by letting us discover it for ourselves.

Miracles are something that we can celebrate and give thanks for, but Scripture hints that they are actually God's least favorite option; he uses a miracle when all else fails. God's favorite means for carrying out his purposes, according to the accounts in the Bible, is to use people. When it comes to getting things done, we are in the top drawer of his toolbox.

SUMMARY

- Bible miracles usually use natural processes or sped-up growth, rather than unnatural methods such as instantaneous movement or materialization.

- Bible miracles have built-in limitations to prevent unwanted side effects such as unending multiplication of food.

- *Proposal:* God prefers to use his creation (especially humans) to do his will, and when he has to employ a miracle he usually likes to use natural processes.

27

▼

Sodom's Natural Disaster

Seismologists can't make accurate predictions yet, though God pre-dicted Sodom's destruction. This is described like a natural process because it couldn't be delayed when Lot dawdled.

Most cities are built in dangerous places. Some are built on lowlands near the coast, where there are natural harbors, but this location puts them in maximum danger from tsunamis, hurricanes, and coastal erosion. Others are built beside rivers at their shallowest points, where they can be easily bridged, but this is also the point most likely to be flooded. And others are built where veins of valuable metals and fuels come close to the surface, but these occur at geological fault lines that are most liable to suffer earthquakes. All this means that natural disasters hit a disproportionate number of cities, and when they do, God often gets the blame.

It's understandable that people might jump to this conclusion because the message of Sodom appears to be that God sends natural disasters to punish people. Sodom was destroyed by some kind of geological activity just after God said he would punish the people—but this isn't the only way to interpret the story.

The text tells us that God and his angels destroyed the city (Gen 19:13, 29), so we reasonably assume that God specifically initiated this disaster. Of course, we can also understand these verses as an affirmation that everything ultimately originates with God. He makes the rain that waters crops and also causes floods; he created an earth containing volcanoes that fertilize fields with their ash, but they also destroy homes. There are clues in the text that this disaster was part of the normal processes on this planet so it was going to happen anyway. In that case, rather than purposely sending the disaster, God used this aspect of his creation to bring punishment, though he also stepped in to carry out a dramatic rescue for anyone who was willing to listen.

SEISMIC EVENT

We don't know exactly what happened. The text says "the LORD rained down burning sulfur ... out of the heavens (Gen 19:24). This suggests a massive volcanic event. There is evidence for earthquake activity in the area, and this may have been associated with liquefaction—when the ground is turned to mud that flows and buries everything in its path. This may have been accompanied by released inflammable gases that burned everything in the area.[1] Our mental image of the disaster has been influenced by the art of John Martin, who toured England with his wall-sized canvas of the destruction of Sodom. For his awed paying viewers, this was as amazing as IMAX is today.[2]

One clue that the disaster was inevitable is that the text clearly suggests that the angels had little control over the destructive forces. When Lot delayed leaving, they couldn't stop or even postpone the disaster; they could only grab the family's

---

1. For a discussion of what actually happened, see Jessica Cecil, "The Destruction of Sodom and Gomorrah," BBC History (TinyURL.com/SodomGomorrahBBC).

2. See John Martin, *Sodom and Gomorrah*, Wikimedia Commons (TinyURL. com/SodomGomorrahPainting).

hands and drag them away from the city (Gen 19:16). They told the family to run fast without looking back, but Lot's wife stood and stared. Perhaps she wanted to see what was happening, or perhaps she was sad at leaving a city that she loved—but she died as a result. We can't assume that this was a punishment. The narrative merely implies that she didn't run away from the danger quickly enough—like the angels had instructed—so she suffered what Lot also feared: "this disaster will overtake me" (19:19). From this it seems clear that the angels couldn't prevent the disaster or protect individuals in the disaster area if they didn't move fast enough.

The angels did not go to Sodom to initiate the destruction, but to discover how many people should be rescued from a destruction that was due to happen. The text records the Lord saying, "I will go down and see if what they have done is as bad as the outcry that has reached me," and the two angels left immediately after he said this (Gen 18:21–22). The people are the focus of Abraham's negotiations (Gen 18:23–33), and it seems that God sent the angels as a test to see if they should be rescued, based on how the angels were treated. Lot gave them hospitality, but late in the night a mob consisting of the men of the city beat on his door, intent on gang-raping them (Gen 19:4–9). God had agreed with Abraham that if there were even ten people in the city who weren't wicked, the whole city would be saved. As it was, the angels could find only one family to rescue.

THE POSSIBILITY OF RESCUE

Another clue that disaster was inevitable is that God had already announced Sodom would be destroyed before talking to Abraham (Gen 18:17)—and presumably God knew this would happen long before the people of Sodom decided to put their city in this geologically rich though also dangerous location.

Abraham's negotiation assumed that the righteous would live or die along with the wicked: "Far be it from you ... to kill the righteous with the wicked" (Gen 18:25). But God had a better plan: to rescue as many as responded to the call to be saved. In the end, their overwhelming sinfulness meant that only a few were evacuated. The warning went out to other families, but they ignored it (Gen 19:14). The disaster was inevitable, but everyone in the city *could* have survived.

How could the angels have saved the whole city if they weren't able to stop the geological catastrophe itself? The answer lies in their instructions to Lot after they'd dispersed the mob by blinding them: they told him to go and warn others who were close to him. Lot duly spent all night trying to persuade his prospective sons-in-law to leave the city, but they only laughed at him. At dawn, the angels called a halt to Lot's efforts, saying that if he and his family didn't leave immediately, the disaster would kill them, too.

The whole city could have been saved. If the men had come to Lot's house to greet his guests instead of to rape them, the angels could have warned them of the impending disaster. Sodom was not large by modern standards—even a major city such as Jericho contained only two or three thousand people. So the message could have quickly spread to every household, which could have spent the night preparing for evacuation at dawn.

REPENTANCE AND JUDGMENT

Jesus used this disaster as an object lesson for those who reject God's warnings about evil. He said that if cities like Tyre and Sodom had repented, they would have been saved. Jesus didn't mean that the physical location wouldn't have been destroyed if the people had repented, because he said that "the land of Sodom" would stand before God at judgment day—that is, the people, not the location (Matt 10:15; 11:23–24). The Sodom that would have been saved was the people—while the physical location was doomed by the natural disaster. Presumably, those who were rescued would have built a new Sodom, just like the survivors of Tyre built a new Tyre near their flattened city.

Another disaster in the Old Testament was the earthquake in the kingdoms of Israel and Judah in about 760 BC (Amos 1:1).[3] Amos prophesied about God's judgment two years before the earthquake happened, so we might assume that God deliberately chose to send it. But there's a problem with this: the prophets didn't say that people living at that time were worse than previous or future generations. Actually, Judah's king at the time was Uzziah (aka Azariah), who was generally good—though he did do some bad things after the time of the earthquake (2 Chr 26:16–20). Perhaps Judah suffered an earthquake aimed at their neighboring half-nation of Israel, ruled by Jeroboam, who was "bad" (2 Kgs 14:24). However, all of Israel's kings were labeled as "bad," and Jeroboam was actually used by God to rescue the people (2 Kgs 14:26–27).

One thing that *was* new during their reigns was wealth. The wise foreign policy of both kings made a lot of people rich (see 2 Chr 26:8–10; 2 Kgs 14:25), and Amos complained that they didn't care about those who remained poor (Amos 2:6–8). This perhaps *is* a clue about the earthquake, because Amos specified that the palaces would be destroyed. However, Amos said they would be destroyed by fire and enemies, not by an earthquake (2:5; 3:11, 15).

These details suggest that God didn't send this earthquake as a specific punishment. Instead, before it occurred, he sent the prophecy in order to try to get people to listen to the accompanying warnings about future judgments. When the prediction

---

3. Amos says Jeroboam II still reigned, and he died in 753 BC.

about a disaster came true, it meant that Amos got everyone's attention. And Zechariah also used this earthquake to make his message about final judgment more vivid for those living in Jerusalem (Zech 14:5). It appears that God used a geological event to present his timeless message in a way that would be remembered and acted on.

Amos' warnings weren't directed at a generation that was more sinful than others, but he warned all generations that God will one day judge us. As with the disaster at Sodom, this interpretation implies that the catastrophic earthquake that hit Jerusalem was going to happen anyway, but God used it to warn people about his anger at sin in general.

Jesus had the same understanding of disasters. He said that those who suffered in the natural and political disasters of his day weren't worse sinners than anyone else. And, like these Old Testament prophets, he used these disasters to warn everyone, saying: "Unless you repent, you too will all perish" (Luke 13:3).

In the story of Sodom, God's rescue plan for those who would listen to him demonstrates his overwhelming desire to save us from what we deserve. Those who listen to Jesus' message will take in the salutary warning.

Disasters are not always sent as specific punishments from the hand of God, but they can all act as a reminder that a real judgment is coming that will be totally just and much more severe. Their purpose is, according to Jesus, to remind us of the good news that God offers an eternity without evil for those who turn to him in repentance.

SUMMARY

- The angels couldn't delay the destruction of Sodom, so they had to grab and drag Lot's family to safety, and they couldn't save Lot's wife, who hung back.

- Saving "the city" does not mean saving the buildings, because Jesus said the city would stand before God's throne—that is, he referred to the people.

- Amos, Zechariah, and Jesus pointed to natural disasters as warnings of God's coming judgment, and not as a punishment of those actually killed by them.

- *Proposal:* God can use natural disasters to punish and to warn, but the Bible does not tell us that he produces specific disasters to do this.

28

▼

Explaining the Exodus Miracles

Attempts to explain these miracles don't work very well, but we aren't wrong to try the Bible itself explains how the Jordan dried up (in a way that was understandable at the time). The most spectacular element in these miracles is their exact timing.

A film crew from *National Geographic* unexpectedly turned up at my workplace. "We've just come from the wind tunnel in the engineering department to witness the Red Sea parting. Now we're here to film the burning bush." After a stunned silence, I remembered seeing Professor Sir Colin Humphreys in the building and realized they wanted him. His professional expertise as a chemical engineer got him a knighthood, and he is equally famous for his work on science and the Bible. As well as writing popular books, he sets himself the goal of publishing his work in peer-reviewed science journals. He has been remarkably successful.

I don't think there is anything wrong with "explaining" miracles by trying to find out how they happened—the Bible itself does this occasionally, as we'll see below—but it *can* spoil their effect. It's rather like explaining a magic trick—as soon as you see how it's done, the mystery and wonder disappear. I can see why the Magic Circle expels members who reveal these secrets. However, when you *do* understand how a trick works, you can end up admiring the ingenuity or dexterous skill of the show-man, who had to create intricate devices and spent many hours practicing in order to create the appearance of magic. Similarly, when we know how God did something, it doesn't necessarily reduce our wonder at his power, because it reveals the mechanisms through which he exerted that power and control.

THE BURNING BUSH

I didn't follow the film crew to watch the bush burning, but I was curious enough to ask Sir Colin at coffee time whether it had survived. He assured me that he hadn't left a burnt stump in the grounds, though he said that it hadn't worked quite as well as he'd hoped—things rarely do when people are filming! The flammable chemical he put on the bush hadn't had enough time to spread thinly. The idea is that the chemical burns slowly and produces a lot of flame, but little of the heat is directed down to the base—so the bush has fire on it, but it doesn't burn.

Was this what Moses saw? Apparently, some desert bushes exude a flammable oil that can be ignited by rare actions such as lightning and then burn like Sir Colin's chemical. Perhaps, instead, the flames were put into Moses' mind, or perhaps God created a special fire-retardant bush and then directed a heavenly flamethrower at it. The problem is that just thinking of these options spoils the whole effect. We lose the wonder and the theological significance—that God wanted to reveal himself to Moses in order to rescue the Israelites from Egypt.

However, according to the Bible text, Moses was just as curious as we are about what was actually happening. It says: "Moses saw that though the bush was on fire it did not burn up. So Moses thought, 'I will go over and see this strange sight—why the bush does not burn up'" (Exod 3:2–3). When he had gotten closer, God called to him, and then Moses hid the bush from his view because he feared looking at God. And yet God hadn't discouraged him from looking—in fact, he had deliberately attracted Moses' attention in this way. God does not mind us looking closely and investigating how he works. We see this elsewhere because the Bible sometimes tells us a remarkable amount about how God works, within the narrow limits of what we can understand.

THE PLAGUES

The plagues that came to Egypt are mostly described in mundane terms. Some of them are awesome, such as the thunderstorms with deadly hail, or the dense dark clouds that caused total darkness. But most of them evince disgust rather than awe: frogs, lice, swarms, cattle disease, and boils. They are all nasty, but not terribly dangerous—except for the hail, when Moses warned everyone to stay indoors (Exod 9:19). The point of these miracles was partly to annoy Pharaoh until he complied, and partly to show by the timing of events that God was in total control. Moses warned when each plague would come, then did something such as waving his staff to start the plague, and finally prayed to God to end it. All this showed that they came from God. So Pharaoh gradually recognized that Israel's God controlled these frightening aspects of nature. It was clearly Israel's God because these plagues didn't happen in Goshen, where the Israelites had their farms (Exod 8:22–23; 9:4).

The final plague is completely different, and it is this one that convinces Pharaoh that he cannot withstand God's will. This not only resulted in massive human death, but also demonstrated God's total control over events by affecting only the eldest son in each household. This miracle stands out from the others, and it is meant to. It was intended to portray what happens when the mercy and patience of God run out. Pharaoh is described as "hard-hearted" (i.e., stubborn), and the theme of God's control is emphasized by saying that God enabled him to remain this stubborn. However, the text also says that Pharaoh hardened his own heart (Exod 9:34–35), which implies that God was merely helping him to keep going down the destructive path he had chosen. Of course, this makes us wonder why God would want Pharaoh to stick to his plan. We can only conclude (as Paul did) that God wanted to glorify himself (Rom 9:22–23)—that is, he wanted to show Israel a miracle they would never forget and that would give them courage in tough times.

These plagues are not portrayed in the language of miracles, except with regard to their timing and their ferocity. We've all experienced gnats and swarms of insects, and many people experience boils, life-threatening hailstones, locust plagues, and livestock diseases. The blood-red river sounds unnatural, but this would also be the way to describe a river swamped by red algae, which, in sufficient concentrations, can kill fish and taste bitter.[1] The Bible text makes clear that all the water in the Nile and drawn from it was affected, but water in boreholes was fine (Exod 7:24). This suggests that water that had not been in contact with the Nile before the problem started was not affected. It would also fit with the idea that this was due to algae, because algal spores would be in any pots of water that had been drawn from the Nile—and would be ready to bloom at the same time—but they would not be in ground water.

Because the Bible text itself provides these clues, I am encouraged to look for this type of explanation in it. Sometimes it even gives an explanation of its own, such as with the

---

1. Red algae closed an Australian beach in 2012. See "Red Algae Bloom Closes Sydney, Australia, Beaches," Huffpost, November 27, 2012 (TinyURL.com/RedAlgalBloom). Rivers have also turned red from other causes such as minerals. See "Red Water," Damage Control (TinyURL.com/RiversTurnedToBlood).

plague of locusts. When Moses stretched out his staff, the locusts didn't appear immediately, but the wind changed direction, and a day later the locusts arrived in that wind (10:13). When Pharaoh begged Moses to pray, "the LORD changed the wind" (10:19) again, and the locusts were removed.

The plagues also follow a natural order. After the Nile waters became uninhabitable, frogs moved inland and even into people's houses and kitchens (8:13). After these died and left piles of rotting corpses (8:14), the country suffered gnats and swarms of larger insects (8:16–32)—as you might expect. These insects landed "on people and animals" (8:17), after which the livestock became diseased, and people suffered boils (9:1–12). These logical progressions are not just created by a modern mind looking for explanations. They are instances of cause and effect we are encouraged to see in the text itself, which says things like, "The frogs died. … They were piled into heaps, and the land reeked" (8:13–14). Not only is God portrayed as able to control nature, but he uses nature in a natural way—albeit with supernatural magnitude.

PARTING THE RED SEA

Parting the Red Sea appears to be something that goes totally against anything seen in nature. We are presented with an image of walls of water that dwarf the Israelites as they hurry across and that later collapse on the Egyptian chariots. This scenario is completely unnatural—but it is also unbiblical. What we see in our minds is the imaginative creation of artists and movie makers.

The Bible text doesn't refer to what we call the "Red Sea," but the "Reed Sea" (Exod 13:18—see the NIV footnote). The Red Sea, which divides lower Egypt from Saudi Arabia, is about two hundred miles wide for most of its length, and two miles deep—which is much more than one night's walk! The narrower Gulf of Suez separates most of Egypt from the Sinai Peninsula. This is about twenty miles wide at the southern end, and it narrows to a river and string of shallow lakes at the northern end.

We can't be sure exactly where Israel crossed this waterway. The text appears to pinpoint the spot by naming nearby locations (see Exod 14:2), but the identities of the various places have been lost in history. This may seem strange given the amount of history that *has* been preserved, but even the former Egyptian capital city of Itjtawy has only just been rediscovered using NASA images, along with thirty-one hundred other settlements, most of which haven't been identified by name.[2] So it isn't surprising that most of the locations on Israel's exodus itinerary (some of which may be no more than an oasis) are no longer identifiable.

However, one very important clue lies in the name the Bible gives to the stretch of water: the Yam Suph, or "Sea of Reeds." We may not know where this is, but the name tells us something very important: there were reeds growing in it, which means it was shallow, at least at the edge. Also, the fact that chariots followed them means that the sides can't have been very steep. This is both a solution and a problem. It makes it more likely that people could cross it, but much less likely that their pursuers would be overwhelmed and drowned by it.

The Bible text solves this problem by stating the method used to allow the Israelites to cross and also to drown the soldiers. It says a strong wind blew all night to part the waters (Exod 14:21). This is something that is perfectly possible with shallow water—as Sir Colin demonstrated to the film crew in a wind-tunnel simulation. Of course, it doesn't exactly create two "walls" of water,

2. See Mark Millmore, "Newsletter 54 Finding the City Itjtawy from Space," *Discovering Egypt*, September 23, 2016 (TinyURL.com/Itjtawy).

to which the text refers (Exod 14:22, 29). The Hebrew word for "wall" is normally used for city walls, so we can forgive those artists and movie directors who have imagined two cliff-like edges of water. However, the same word is also used for other barriers, such as when David's men gave protection to shepherds, who described them as "a wall around us" (1 Sam 25:16). So a wall of water could refer to whatever held that water back and formed a visible edge where the water stopped.

But when the wind stopped in the morning so that the waters could flow again, would this overwhelm and drown the soldiers? The wind-tunnel experiments confirm what is seen occasionally in nature: when water has been held back in this way and is suddenly released, it sweeps forward with a high wave driven by all the pent-up energy of the water behind it. This would have crashed into the soldiers like water from a burst dam, so it is unsurprising that they were totally overwhelmed and all drowned.

I'm afraid that I do prefer Cecil B. DeMille's portrayal, because it seems much more exciting. But our imagination should be guided by what the Bible actually says.

CROSSING THE JORDAN

There is one miracle from Israel's journey to Canaan where we don't just get a clue about how it was done: the crossing of the Jordan is explained clearly for anyone with a little local knowledge. The Israelites had to cross this river forty years after the exodus because it separated the wilderness from the land that was going to be their home. The timing was really bad because they arrived during the spring floods, when the river was moving fast and overflowing its banks (Josh 3:15). The priests carrying the ark of the covenant were told to walk in front and stand in the middle of the river until everyone had crossed. So they walked toward the fast-flowing river, and when they reached it, the water simply stopped arriving. The text says that "the water from upstream stopped flowing. It piled up in a heap a great distance away, at a town called Adam in the vicinity of Zarethan, while the water flowing down to the Sea of the Arabah (that is, the Dead Sea) was completely cut off" (Josh 3:16).

Someone who knows the area would know that when the Jordan passes near the town of Adam (modern-day Damiya, eighteen miles north of their crossing), it bends around a steep slope of loose mud and stones. Every now and then a section of the steep bank collapses and dams the river; then, after several hours, the water breaks through and pushes the mud aside. This is a very rare event—it has only been recorded in 1927, 1906, 1834, 1546, 1267, and 1160, though no doubt it has occurred several more times without being noted—but the possibility is obvious to anyone who sees the site.[3] This account was first written for people who knew the area, so for them this wasn't merely a description of what happened but a full explanation.

By telling us this, the Bible text is emphasizing that the miracle lay in the timing. This is confirmed by the way the text describes the event: "as soon as the priests who carried the ark reached the Jordan and their feet touched the water's edge, the water from upstream stopped flowing" (Josh 3:15–16). And then it explains how it happened by telling the reader the location where it was cut off.

---

3. See Bryant G. Wood, "Did the Israelites Conquer Jericho? A New Look at the Archaeological Evidence," *Biblical Archaeology Review* 16 (1990): 44–58 (TinyURL.com/JerichoArchaeology).

In the end, it is all right to seek explanations of miracles, partly because the Bible text itself encourages us to look for them and partly because it shows that God is able to control the real world that I live in. If the exodus was a totally extraordinary event—that is, one that looked like something from a fantasy novel—then this would make God's activity remote from my life. But when I see that God is manipulating the same world that I live in and using the forces that he, as Creator, has made, then to me this brings his activity much closer to home. I doubt that God will ever send winds or landslides to dry up a water-way for me to cross, but he may well manipulate the weather in ways that benefit me.

This doesn't mean that I want God to change the weather or control plagues of insects whenever I ask. I don't expect this because I'm not important enough, and changes in a weather system affect a lot more people than me. Also, I don't expect it to happen often for other people, because the Bible suggests that God works like this only occasionally. We read that "the LORD drove the sea back with a strong east wind" (Exod 14:21), and he "made an east wind blow across the land" (Exod 10:13). This shows us God stepping in at key points to change things. We shouldn't infer from this that he manipulates every detail minute by minute. He has created his universe to work well, and most of the time it does. However, many flaws were introduced through our sin, so sometimes, as these texts show, God needs to step in and take control. Most of the time we can praise him for his faithfulness in creating a world that runs predictably. But occasionally there is no better explanation than to say that God has stepped in, and it's a miracle—even if we can "explain" how it happened.

SUMMARY

- Moses was curious about how the burning bush worked, and our curiosity about how other miracles work is encouraged by details given in the text.

- The plagues of Exodus follow a logical sequence, and hints in the text encourage us to regard each one as the cause of the next, with miraculous timing.

- The parting of the "Red Sea" is understandable if this is indeed the Sea of Reeds (as the text says), and the parting of the Jordan is explained by the text itself.

- *Proposal:* God's miraculous interventions are seen in the *timing* and *placement* of these events: the plagues happened exactly when Moses said and didn't extend to the homes of Israelites, and waters parted exactly when and where Israel needed.

29

▼

Food in the Wilderness

The Israelites lived in the wilderness for forty years. This clearly involved miracles, but these did not include providing all their food and water—because other nations were managing to live there too.

When the pilgrim fathers arrived in America, the native population had to show them how to survive in a very different type of landscape from the one they had left behind. And for the first year, before they got settled, the natives fed them something that their descendants have never stopped being thankful for. But when the Israelites suddenly found themselves in the wilderness of Sinai, they didn't find friendly new neighbors to help them out.

There is, of course, uncertainty about the number of Israelites who escaped from Egypt into the wilderness, but that won't be dealt with here. Here we consider the nature of the wilderness they lived in and what kinds of miracles they needed. Israel wasn't the only nation living there, so, like the pilgrim fathers, they knew it must be possible to survive in this new environment. The Bible text suggests they did just that, though they sometimes needed extra help.

The other nations weren't keen to have competitors for the limited resources. So, soon after the Israelites arrived, they met and fought with the Amalekites. Israel was only able to win while Moses was praying (Exod 17:11–13), which suggests that the Amalekite army was comparable to the size of Israel's—so these nations were about the same size. These Amalekites were local, living "in the Negev" (i.e., in the wilderness, Num 13:29), and there was another group of Amalekites who lived on the southern edge of Canaan (Num 14:43)—or perhaps there were small groups throughout the area. They attacked because these Israelites were encroaching on their land.

The Amalekites weren't the only ones living in the wilderness, because soon after they were defeated, some Midianites came to visit the Israelites. This was a happier encounter because one of them was Moses' father-in-law (Exod 18:1–9). When Moses had previously fled Egypt on his own, after he had killed an Egyptian, he had run away to "the land of Midian," where he married a Midianite: Zipporah. It was while looking after her father's flock that he'd seen the burning bush—so the land of Midian presumably included the southern wilderness area of Mount Sinai (Exod 2:15–22; 3:1–2).

We don't know who else was living in this wilderness, but it clearly wasn't empty, and presumably it wasn't as barren as it is now. It supported a large number of people and their animals before Israel arrived, and at least one of these nations (the Amalekites) was comparable in size to Israel.

WILDLIFE

Petroglyphs (ancient carvings on rocks) portray a lush wildlife in this Sinai wilderness. Thousands have been found, though their existence is not publicized because the few that have been signposted are now spoiled with graffiti. Various animals are depicted in them, especially the ibex, which must have been relatively common in the area.[1] Clearly it was not always a wilderness.

Paleobotanists have now found that this wilderness (i.e., the modern Negev) was indeed occasionally fertile, and these periods are now identified. Hendrik Bruins of the University of the Negev recently collected carbon-14 dates from archaeological animal feces and burned food scraps. He identified a fertile period spanning from the end of the late Bronze Age to the early Iron Age (about 1600–950 BC)—which includes the period that Israel lived there for forty years.[2]

In the Bible, this area is referred to by the name Negev (meaning "the south") and the word *midbar*—which is related to the verb "to pasture." Although the etymology of *midbar* implies that plants and animals flourished there, it is normally translated "wilderness" because it did not include human settlements such as towns—only a few ranch houses.

However, later in Israel's history, the meaning of the word *midbar* changed. When the later prophets use this word, it tends to mean a "desert." Isaiah contrasted *midbar* with words such as "watered," "fruitful," and "inhabited," and he calls it "a land of terror" (Isa 14:17; 21:1; 27:10; 32:15; 35:1, 6). Jeremiah says the man who turns from God will "dwell in the parched places of the desert [*midbar*] ... where no one lives" (Jer 17:6). Notice that the NIV normally translates *midbar* as "wilderness" in the earlier books but translates it as "desert" when the meaning changed. This change reflects the fact that the Negev went into decline

---

1. See Uzi Avner, Liora Horwitz, and Wayne Horowitz, "Symbolism of the Ibex Motif in Negev Rock Art," *Journal of Arid Environments* 143 (December 2016) (TinyURL.com/NegevIbex).

2. See Hendrik J. Bruins and Johannes van der Plicht, "Dating of Iron Age Agriculture in the Negev Highlands," *Radiocarbon* 59, no. 4 (August 2017): 1233–39 (TinyURL.com/Bruins-Negev).

environmentally, probably due to shifting patterns of climate. It didn't become fertile again until the late Roman period, though a few hundred years later it declined again.

So the area where Israel lived for forty years wasn't a deadly desert—though it wasn't a garden, either. It was an area occupied mainly by flocks, herders, and their families, with few fixed settlements. Therefore, the land had vegetation for Israel's herds, and it was possible for large numbers of people to live there, but it wasn't easy.

GOD'S TIMING

This explains the fact that the miracles of food and water recorded in the Bible occur mostly when they first arrived in the wilderness or when they traveled to new locations where they didn't yet know the water sources. The timetable went like this:

- Three days into the journey, "bitter" water was made drinkable at Marah (Exod 15:22-25).

- They stayed a few weeks at Elim, which had a lot of water (Exod 15:27-16:1).

- They started out for Sinai, but they needed food, so manna fell (Exod 16:1-36).

- A few days later they needed water, and a stream poured from a rock (Exod 17:1-7).

- They spent about a year at Sinai, receiving the law and building the Tabernacle (Num 10:11).

- Having gotten moving again, they complained the manna was boring, so quails arrived (Num 11:4-9, 18-23, 31-32).

- Right at the end of their travels, in the fortieth year, they gathered at Kadesh (ready to enter Canaan) and needed water again, so they got another stream from a rock (Num 20:1–13; for the year, compare 20:28 with 33:38).

It appears that they only needed water on three occasions: at the very start of their journey, when they knew nothing about this wilderness; when they started their major journey to Sinai across strange country; and right at the end. By the end of forty years, we'd expect they would know where to find water, but perhaps they were now all gathered together in a tighter encampment, ready to cross hostile territory, so they could not forage for water so effectively.

WATER FROM THE ROCK

On two occasions, at Meribah and later at Kadesh, water flowed from a rock Moses had struck. The ancient rabbis imagined a single isolated rock that rolled through the wilderness, following them and providing a constant source of water. Paul refers to this image without saying he believed it really happened (1 Cor 10:4). There is nothing in the text to imply the same rock was involved in both places.

It is likely that the water streamed from a rock face at the base of a large block of higher land. Higher land often has a water table that breaks out as a spring in the rock face at the edge. This is why Ancestral Puebloans built homes on the cliff edges of high plateaus such as the Mesa Verde in Colorado, where they could collect the water that came out of the rock face and also access the pastures at the top.[3]

---

3. See Kenneth R. Wright, "Ancestral Puebloan Water Handling," *Lakeline*

Perhaps Moses was at the bottom of a rock face, and by striking the exact spot he released a previously untapped water table. This water would continue to flow, possibly indefinitely if the outflow was matched by periodic rainfall in the higher area. So the miracle consisted of God showing Moses exactly where to hit the rock in order to release this water when it was needed on these two occasions.

By contrast, the manna was constantly provided. It first appeared when the Israelites set out for Sinai in Exodus 16, and by the time they left Sinai a year later, they complained they were bored with it. It finally stopped when they reached Jericho (Josh 5:12). On the occasion they complained about the manna, God promised them meat "until it comes out of your nostrils and you loathe it" (Num 11:20), and soon after the camp was covered in quail.

On a holiday in Malta I was surprised to find the southern coastal areas dotted with small huts no bigger than a latrine. I later realized these were hides—not for bird watching but bird shooting. Malta is the only place in Europe that still allows a twenty-day season for quail shooting—it is in April, when the birds land exhausted on their way from Africa to Europe.[4] About seven thousand people register every year for this sport, which sounds to me as easy as a turkey shoot because the birds are trying to rest.

We don't now know whether quail used to land regularly in the Negev during the more fertile time when Israel was there, but this is certainly possible. In that case, it was a miracle of timing in that they arrived just after God had promised them. Quail normally migrate in April, which is roughly Passover

---

(Winter 2008): 23–28 (TinyURL.com/MesaVerdeWater).
    4. See "Hunting," Birdlife Malta (TinyURL.com/QuailsMalta).

time—that is, the first month. These quail arrived at the end of the second month (Num 10:11), but this may still have been the normal time for these particular quail. The Jewish calendar wanders somewhat because it uses lunar months of 28.5 days each and periodically corrects itself by adding an extra month—which explains why Passover and Easter are so movable. It is therefore likely that this occurred at the normal time for migration, but the calendar was a little misadjusted.

The curious expression "two cubits deep" (Num 11:31) probably doesn't mean they were lying on top of each other to the depth of one meter, but it may refer to the fact that they were exhausted and flying just above the ground, so they were easily caught.[5] The Israelites ate quail for a month (Num 11:19-20), which is about the length of the quail-shooting season on Malta. The quantity and the timing were extraordinary—and can certainly be described as miraculous, even though we can suggest a mechanism for this miracle.[6]

MANNA, MANNA

In contrast, manna is totally mysterious—though there have been several suggestions of natural phenomena that it might be connected with. The Bible describes it as white, like coriander seed or resin, and says that it settled with the dew and "melted" in the full sun. It tasted sweetish and also savory like olive oil, and it could be boiled or ground into flour and baked. But it didn't store well—it soon smelled and attracted maggots (Exod 16:20-23, 31; Num 11:7-9). This is similar to various identifiable phenomena: tiny white mushrooms that pop up when dew

---

5. This is suggested by Josephus in *Antiquities of the Jews* 3.1.5 (TinyURL.com/JosephusQuails).

6. See chap. 28, "Explaining the Exodus Miracles."

moistens the land, exudates from insects (as found in tamarisk trees or the "Manna of Iran" found on bushes), exudates from trees themselves (such as the white "Manna Ash" found in Iraq and Iran), and others.[7]

The problem with all of these phenomena is that they are short-lived or occur only in tiny quantities, so they can't have been a natural source of food for the nation during their forty years of wandering. Whatever it was, Israel considered it unusual and didn't have a name for it; they called it *man-ah* (meaning "What [is] it?"), so it wasn't merely large quantities of something that normally occurred.

None of these ideas concerning manna completely emulate what is described in the Bible narratives, but they do help us to see that the miracles in the wilderness fit into the pattern found throughout the Bible. Instead of materializing the food or water that was needed, God used his creation to supply it. In the case of manna, we still don't know what part of his creation he used to produce it or what kind of food was produced. However, it arrived alongside the natural phenomenon of dew, had to be collected in early morning, and needed to be processed before it was edible—so it wasn't simply a food handout at mealtimes.

So the water and quail were likely from normal sources, but the timing and quantity were miraculous. The water came from a rock face, which is where streams normally do break out, but Moses knew exactly where to strike the rock in order to release an untapped water table. Similarly, the quail arrived at the expected time, though in unexpectedly large quantities and sufficiently exhausted to be caught easily—and also in exactly the right place, where Israel was camped.

---

7. See Roger S. Wotton, "What Was Manna?," *Opticon1826* 9 (Autumn 2010) (TinyURL.com/WottonManna).

Personally, I'm still left with the uneasy feeling that the miracles are diminished somewhat when we understand some of the mechanisms behind them. However, I realize that this is due to my failure to appreciate the *way* that God works. I've read and seen too much science fiction and fantasy, where amazing things happen by completely alien means. But the God of the Bible is the one who created *this* world, so we shouldn't expect his acts to appear alien. We expect them to be homely but awesome. That is, they should be similar at least in some ways to actions that are normal in creation, though done at a special time, or in extraordinary quantities, or amazingly quickly. And that is how we see God working in the Bible.

SUMMARY

- Other similar-sized nations were already living in the wilderness when Israel arrived, so it was not impossible to live there.

- Water normally does break out from rock faces around an upland area, and migrating quail normally arrive exhausted and easy to catch.

- Various substances that fit the description of manna do arise naturally, though not in the large quantities described.

- *Proposal:* The wilderness miracles are extraordinary in terms of timing and quantity, but not necessarily extraordinarily different from phenomena that still occur naturally.

30

▼

Predicting the Future
by the Stars

Astronomers can predict heavenly signs foretold by the Bible, such as blood moons, and the wise men predicted Christ's birth. Can we predict the future using the Bible or the stars?

N owadays, an Old Testament prophet might well make it onto the nation's wealthiest people list, because reliably predicting the price of corn or oil can net you a fortune trading in stock market futures. Elisha correctly predicted a fall in corn prices (2 Kgs 7:1), so in the business world of today he could have been a rich man. The book of Revelation has some similar commodity price predictions that immediately precede the occurrence of some "blood moons" (Rev 6:6, 12). Are you tempted to look up the astronomy charts to work out the timing?

Horoscopes and star charts are still incredibly important in some Eastern cultures, as well as being popular ("just for fun") in the West. Somehow we can't get it out of our minds that our destiny is tied up with those lights that shimmer above us. In ancient days, when stars and planets were thought to be capricious gods, this did make some kind of sense. The surprising thing is that this belief continued even after Mesopotamian astronomers put together a huge dataset of observations and started accurately predicting heavenly events. Instead of deciding that the heavenly bodies clearly weren't unpredictable divinities, they concluded that this information could be used to predict good and bad luck.

For example, they expected a solar eclipse to bring extreme bad luck, especially for the ruler. So when the astronomers said that one was due, a substitute was put on the throne to rule just for that day, so that the expected bad fortune would fall on him rather than on the king. The next day they sacrificed the stand-in to ensure that the full bad luck of the eclipse fell on him. One fortunate individual, who happened to be a gardener, escaped being sacrificed because the real king died on that same day from drinking soup that was too hot—so the substitute carried on reigning.[1]

STAR OF BETHLEHEM

The magi—usually translated the "wise men"—came from Mesopotamia to see Jesus. Some people regard their use of the stars as a justification for using horoscopes—after all, they did appear to predict the future by looking at astronomical events. However, this idea doesn't stand up to much scrutiny.

There are two main theories concerning what they saw: either a comet or a conjunction of planets. Combining the two creates a compelling account. The planets Jupiter and Saturn were conjoined (that is, they were very close to each other) in the constellation of Pisces three times in 7 BC, and then again in 6 BC along with Mars. These were followed by a comet that was visible for seventy days in 5 BC according to ancient Chinese records. These events would be very significant for the magi,

---

1. See Sarah Graff, "The Solar Eclipse and the Substitute King," *Now at the Met* (TinyURL.com/SubstituteKing).

who believed conjunctions of Saturn and Jupiter portended important events, and associated Pisces particularly with the country of Israel.[2]

At this point we have to ask whether the planets and stars actually influence life on earth (as astrologers claim) or whether God planned Jesus' birth to come at a time that the magi (and a few others) would have regarded as significant. Johannes Kepler saw these same planetary conjunctions when they occurred again in 1604, and he calculated that this event occurs every 805 years. His own sighting was followed by the appearance of a supernova, which created a bright new star in the sky—the second-brightest supernova in history. And yet these celestial events in Kepler's day didn't accompany anything close to the importance of the birth of Christ. Kepler himself felt that something significant *did* happen every 805 years: Moses was born in 1617 BC, Isaiah in 812 BC, the reign of Charlemagne began in 799 AD, and the Reformation in 1604. Unfortunately, all these dates are wrong: the birth of Moses occurred three centuries later than Kepler "predicted" by the stars, Isaiah about one century earlier, the coronation of Charlemagne a year later, and the Reformation is generally dated from the time of Luther's Ninety-Five Theses in 1517 or a host of other events, none of which occurred in 1604.

Just because Jesus' birth was timed to coincide with signs that some would regard as significant does not mean that they *produced* that birth or predicted it, because similar signs do not produce other equally significant events on other occasions. This doesn't put off astrologers, because it is usually possible

2. See Colin J. Humphreys, "The Star of Bethlehem, a Comet in 5 BC, and the Date of the Birth of Christ," *Quarterly Journal of the Royal Astronomical Society* 32 (1991): 389–407 (TinyURL.com/StarMagi).

to find *something* that has occurred that could be tied to a celestial event. So throughout history, the stars have been studied to see whether they can reveal some secrets about the progress or future of the world.

PREDICTING ASTRONOMICAL EVENTS

The very first mechanical calculating device, the Antikythera mechanism, was invented to make astronomical predictions. This complex matrix of bronze cogs and dials included a special function for predicting red lunar eclipses. It was probably based on a design by Archimedes from the third century BC. In about 60 BC, it was lost in a shipwreck on the way to Rome and was recovered from the seabed in 1901—though its purpose wasn't known until X-ray tomography revealed its internal structure.[3]

Like many inventions today, this kind of device had military applications. A terrible Greek naval disaster occurred in 413 BC at the time of a lunar eclipse, which encouraged the belief that military men could take advantage of heavenly portents. In 585 BC Greek mathematician Thales was able to warn the embattled Lydians that a solar eclipse was due. They could have used this for military advantage in a battle with their long-term enemies, the Medes, by preparing for the sudden darkness that they knew would occur—their unprepared enemy could have been easily defeated in the confusion. But instead it appears that they used it to engineer a lasting peace. When the expected darkness interrupted the fighting, they declared that the gods were demanding an end to the war.[4]

---

3. See Wikipedia, "Antikythera Mechanism" (TinyURL.com/StarClock).

4. See Wikipedia, "Eclipse of Thales" (TinyURL.com/ThalesEclipse). Unsurprisingly, there are other theories. See Natasha Frost, "Was the First Eclipse Prediction an Act of Genius, a Brilliant Mistake, or Dumb Luck?," Atlas Obscura (2017) (TinyURL.com/ThalesMystery).

Even as late as 1504, Columbus was able to use a similar trick to imply that God was on his side. He had been stranded in Jamaica for some time, and the islanders were fed up with having to feed his unruly men. Realizing that he had to gain the upper hand, he consulted his seaman's almanac and discovered that there was going to be a red moon. He announced to the islanders that the moon would show God's anger about their reluctance to feed his men anymore. When the earth's shadow fell across the moon so that it turned blood-red, the islanders started wailing, begging forgiveness, and running to bring food.[5]

BLOOD MOONS

Few people today are bothered about blood moons—except for some Christians. This is because the Bible has a handful of predictions involving the moon turning to blood, some of which relate to Jesus' second coming. Blood moons by themselves happen relatively frequently—about every two years on average. However, a few years ago something less common occurred: a lunar tetrad—that is, a group of four lunar eclipses separated by six-month intervals. This tetrad spanned from 2014 until the last one on September 28, 2015. In fact, this century is special because it contains eight such tetrads, from 2003/2004 until 2090/2091.

Some preachers caused excitement by pointing out that the eclipses happening in 2014/2015 were all falling on Jewish festivals: the ones in April 2014 and 2015 on the first day of Passover, and the two in September on the first day of Tabernacles. This was considered so awesome that I was asked by a Christian magazine to predict what would happen in the light of Bible prophecy. Unfortunately, I had to disappoint readers by explaining that this precise pattern is relatively common because alignment

---

5. See Wikipedia, "March 1504 Lunar Eclipse" (TinyURL.com/1504Eclipse).

with Jewish festivals occurs on one in six of these blood moon tetrads. The reason is that Passover and Tabernacles always occur at full moon and are always six lunar months apart, and blood moons also always occur at full moon, and when they occur in a tetrad they are always six months apart. In fact, it would be more significant if *none* of the eight tetrads this century had lined up with these festivals. Perhaps the most significant thing about this particular tetrad is that all four were visible in the US, so a lot of American believers were aware of them.

In the Bible, darkened or blood-red moons are generally mentioned along with overwhelming destruction from God: on Judah (Joel 2:10, 31), on Egypt (Ezek 32:7), on Babylon (Isa 13:10), and on "the kings on the earth" (Isa 24:21–23). Other verses that link a blood moon with the final "Day of the LORD" (Joel 2:10; 3:15, Isa 13:10) were cited by Jesus and Peter when describing the second coming (Matt 24:29 and parallels; Acts 2:20). In Jesus' description, these final blood moons occur after "the tribulation of those days" and immediately before "the Son of man coming on the clouds" (Matt 24:29–30).

Does this mean that astronomical predictions could help us determine likely windows of time when Jesus' return will happen? Unfortunately (or perhaps fortunately), these biblical descriptions are likely to have nothing to do with actual astronomic phenomena. Phrases such as "the moon will turn to blood" were part of the shock-and-awe language of ancient divine warfare, along with the heavens being rolled up like a scroll and stars falling out of the sky (Isa 34:4; Matt 24:29; Rev 6:14). An equivalent modern threat would be, "We will flatten all your cities with mushroom clouds that darken the sun and turn the moon red." Someone who isn't used to our idioms would be confused to find that bombed cities aren't actually flat and that no fungi are involved—it is just our language of destruction. In the same way, moons turned to blood are part of the Hebrew language of destruction.

HOW BIBLE PROPHECY WORKS

I don't believe that Bible prophecy is given to us as a method for predicting the future—it does foretell the future accurately, but its purpose is not to help people know future timing in advance. Rather, it is a means of giving comfort to those who will be going through those events, because they will be able to recognize their own days in retrospect and realize that God knew what would happen in advance. If someone had tried to use Psalm 22 to predict the trials of the Messiah, they would have assumed he'd have to face angry bulls and lions before being ravaged by dogs, perhaps in a Roman arena (read Ps 22:12–13, 16). But after the event, we can recognize which parts of this psalm are metaphorical and which ones are surprisingly literal. Who would have guessed that his sufferings involved specific literal injuries to his hands and feet or that the execution method involved hanging in the sun and becoming dehydrated (vv. 15–16)? Someone trying to use this psalm to predict the future would have gotten things hopelessly wrong, but after the event we can recognize that it foretold what would happen with amazing accuracy.

The early church was able to take comfort in such prophecies after Jesus was killed. In fact, Jesus himself used prophecy in this kind of way: when talking on the road to Emmaus, "beginning with Moses and all the Prophets, he explained to them what was said in all the Scriptures concerning himself" (Luke 24:27).

When the predicted disasters occur, we'll be able to realize that God knew all about it and had a remedy planned, because we will recognize the prophecies. But we should only expect this to work in retrospect. Too many people have made fools of themselves by trying to predict from the Bible what will happen—and have ended up making the Bible look foolish to those who listened to them.

Some preachers who thought that the blood moons of 2014/2015 were especially significant regarded Islamist terrorism as part of the "great tribulation, such as has not been from the beginning of the world until now, no, and never will be"—because this precedes the blood moons just before Jesus' second coming (Matt 24:21 ESV). But, as usual, this turned out to be a false alarm.

We humans are always on the lookout for danger, and this is a healthy and life-sustaining trait so long as we recognize it. Even without stars, moons, or horoscopes, we can find the potential for predicting disaster. When the year 2000 came along, there was a sophisticated version of millennial apprehension: the Y2K bug. The fear was that older computers weren't programmed to understand years beyond 1999, so they might have gotten confused when that year ended. It was predicted that bank safes wouldn't open, billing would go wrong, medical equipment would stop, planes would fall out of the sky, and intercontinental missiles would fire on their own. Christian leaders advised stocking up food, and Jerry Falwell even suggested buying a few guns, as he himself had done, to "persuade others not to mess with us."[6] I felt particularly sorry for Steve Hewitt, the editor of *Christian Computing Magazine*, who had enough specialist knowledge to know that this was hype. He was the voice of sanity when many well-known preachers were stoking this fear, but fellow Christians severely criticized him for ignoring the Bible message about coming disasters.[7]

---

6. See Rob Boston, "Apocalypse Now?," *Church and State* (1999) (TinyURL.com/EndIsNighY2K).

7. See Dave Hunt, "Y2K the Real Disaster," *The Berean Call*, May 1, 1999 (TinyURL.com/HuntHewittY2K).

Many such crises have come and gone, and I'm sure that the next one will soon turn up. When we look up to the stars or stare into the future, we need to look to the Creator of those hosts, who has proclaimed that he is bringing about a good future. Yes, he has also given us warning of severe trouble on the way—not so that we can work out exactly what and when it will happen, but so that we won't lose heart or faith when it does.

SUMMARY

- The "star of Bethlehem" was probably an event that recurs every 805 years, but it was only significant once.

- Predicting eclipses and blood moons is interesting, but this cannot tell us about the future.

- Bible prophecies, like the ones predicting the Messiah, are accurate but can only be recognized in retrospect.

- *Proposal:* God provides predictions of troubles in the future so that those who will suffer them know that he is still in control—not so that we can fore-tell the future.

31

Can a Virgin Birth
Produce a Real Man?

Spontaneous virgin birth is scientifically very unlikely—although not impossible. Theologically it is more problematic: How can Jesus be a natural man if he is born by unnatural means? One proposal helps to solve both sets of difficulties.

The first scientifically recorded human virgin birth almost happened in 2004, though the Korean team led by Hwang Woo-Suk didn't let it come to term. However, he didn't publicize this fact because he was trying to fraudulently win the race to produce the first stem cells from a cloned human embryo. To do this, he had to create a clone, but he found it simpler to perform the first human parthenogenesis ("virgin birth"). He stimulated an egg to divide and start growing by itself—and it worked. By the time his fraud was uncovered, another team had done what he'd set out to do. He was publicly shamed for claiming what he hadn't achieved. However, what he had achieved was successfully initiating a "virgin birth."[1] Growing this kind of human life

---

1. See Christopher Williams, "Stem Cell Fraudster Made 'Virgin Birth' Breakthrough," *The Register*, August 3, 2007 (TinyURL.com/HwangHoax).

beyond a few days is ethically forbidden throughout the world, but we now know that it may not be too difficult.

Parthenogenesis—the birth of an animal without involving a father—is a normal form of reproduction in some animals such as goblin spiders, the New Zealand mud snail, freshwater guppies, whiptail lizards, and the Komodo dragon. It also occurs in domesticated turkeys, where live chicks are occasionally hatched in an all-female population. It may also happen among wild turkeys, but this is difficult to demonstrate without very intensive observation—a limitation that also applies to other species—so it may be more common than we know. No natural parthenogenesis has been observed among mammals, although it has been induced in rabbits, mice, and monkeys. This rarely produces live births, although some academics have suggested that parthenogenesis may have occasionally succeeded naturally even among humans.[2]

So, from a scientific point of view, a virgin birth is not impossible—merely extremely unlikely—and God could presumably perform the minor manipulations necessary to make a parthenogenetic fetus develop correctly. Normally, one would expect this to result in a female baby, though a male is a statistical possibility—as discussed below. The probability of this happening by accident is so small that we wouldn't expect it at any point in human history, let alone at the precise moment when the Messiah was due to be born or to parents who were anticipating it. It is not something we could envisage happening without divine intervention—which is what makes it a miracle. But

---

2. See Wikipedia, "Parthenogenesis" (TinyURL.com/WikiPartheno), and Gabriel Jose de Carlia and Tiago Campos Pereira, "On Human Parthenogenesis," *Medical Hypotheses* 106 (September 2017): 57–60 (TinyURL.com/HumanPartheno).

equally, it would not break any scientifically discovered laws of what is possible.

FULLY HUMAN

The theological problem is potentially a much greater issue than any scientific improbabilities. The difficulty is that a virgin birth separates Jesus from "normal" humanity, making him different from everyone else. This is an issue because theologians recognized from a very early date that the incarnation of Jesus as a real human was a key factor in salvation. That is, in order to save humans, Jesus had to become a human—a real human.

Irenaeus first enunciated this in the second century AD when some people said that Jesus had a divine mind but not a fully human one. He argued against this, saying that Jesus must have had a human mind; otherwise our minds wouldn't be saved along with the rest of us. He said, "To destroy sin, and redeem man ... He should Himself be made that very same thing which he was, that is, man."[3] Ephrem the Syrian echoed this theme in the fourth century, saying, "He descended and became one of us that we might become heavenly."[4] This understanding was encapsulated most memorably by Gregory of Nazianzus, also in the fourth century, who summarized it in this way: "That which He has not assumed He has not healed; but that which is united to His Godhead is also saved."[5] In other words, Jesus had to be incarnated with all the aspects of a full human in order that every part of us could be saved.

---

3. Irenaeus, *Against Heresies* 3.18.7 (TinyURL.com/IrenausFullyMan).

4. Ephrem the Syrian, *Hymns on Nativity* 3:16, cited in Jung Kim, "Catechesis and Mystagogy in St. Ephrem the Syrian" (ThD diss., Boston University, 2013), 211 (TinyURL.com/EphremHeavenly).

5. Gregory Nazianzen, "To Cledonius the Priest against Apollinarius," *Epistle 101* (TinyURL.com/GregoryN-101).

Irenaeus didn't consider Jesus' virgin birth to be problematic because he felt that as long as Jesus faced all the same temptations we do, then he represented all of humanity.[6] However, his special form of birth is clearly something that sets Jesus apart. More recent theologians have pointed out that Jesus didn't share some important aspects of humanity, and therefore he might be said to not understand or represent them—including being female and being disabled.[7]

I don't think that Jesus could realistically be expected to represent *every* strata and state of humanity. However, he shared an amazingly wide gamut of our human existence. Jesus suffered poverty, persecution, and, perhaps, racial profiling at the hands of the Romans. He experienced physical labor, emotional and physical pain, and torture. It is surely unreasonable to suggest that he didn't represent everyone because he wasn't both male and female, or that he had to experience every type of human condition, such as paralysis, blindness, or mental disability. He could still represent all of humanity by being fully human. Having said that, one way in which God could have caused the virgin birth may actually make Jesus even more representative of all humans—as we will see below.

XX MEN

One characteristic of parthenogenesis is that it normally results in the birth of females. This is because females have two X chromosomes, while males have an X and a Y. So an egg will always have an X chromosome, while sperms can either contain an X or a Y chromosome. Therefore, if a female egg is stimulated to

---

6. Irenaeus, *Against Heresies* 3.19.3 (TinyURL.com/Irenaeus3-19).

7. For an erudite and brief exploration, see Maria Gwyn McDowell, "Choose, Francis: Incarnation or Imago Dei?," Women in Theology, May 14, 2016 (TinyURL.com/McDowell-Incarnation).

form an embryo by parthenogenesis, the embryo will only have X chromosomes because there is no Y available without a sperm. This means that all parthenogenesis should result in females—as indeed normally happens.

However, there is a condition where someone with XX chromosomes is actually born a male. This happens in about one in twenty thousand male births—which means that about eight thousand men living in the US today have XX chromosomes, like women do. We don't hear much about this because they are unlikely to tell their friends and, actually, they may not even know about it themselves because they often look identical to other men. Some are born with sexual ambiguity, so their condition is diagnosed at birth, but it may not be discovered until later, during tests for other things such as abnormal development or infertility.[8]

Some, however, are never diagnosed, because they may have normal levels of testosterone so that they look and feel like ordinary men. The XX-male syndrome usually results by the process of gene "crossover"—that is, the swapping of the testosterone gene SRY, which is on the Y chromosome, with a very similar gene that is on the X chromosome, during the production of sperm. In 10 percent of cases, however, it occurs by the mutation of that gene which is already on the X chromosome in the sperm or egg, into the form of male SRY. The International Olympic Committee is aware of this problem, so they now define males by the amount of testosterone produced rather than relying on X and Y chromosomes.[9]

You have probably guessed where this is going: the simplest way that God could produce a male offspring by parthenogenesis

---

8. See Wikipedia, "XX Male Syndrome" (TinyURL.com/WikiXXMale).

9. See Wikipedia, "Sex Verification in Sports" (TinyURL.com/SportGender).

was by creating an XX-male. This would never happen by itself because the improbabilities are just too extraordinary. Parthenogenic birth has a vanishingly small probability of occurring among humans, and the extra improbability that mutations would cause this XX-male syndrome makes it even less likely. In fact, we should conclude that it would never happen—except by a miracle.

But why, in any case, would God use this kind of mechanism based on normal human genetics? He could simply give Mary a fertilized egg containing DNA with any pattern of his choosing. In this way, Jesus could have been born looking like the blue-eyed Scandinavian envisioned in some modern art, or with the chiseled Roman bone structure depicted by early Christian artists. But as the early theologians pointed out, this would mean that Jesus was not really related to humanity. The whole point of being born from Mary was that he inherited the full human condition—including all our temptations and imperfections—as well as the Jewish royal genetic line.

GOD USES HIS CREATION

The other reason I think God didn't use a more interventionist approach is that (as I have pointed out throughout this book) he prefers using his own creation to carry out his purposes. After all, that's why he created it. If, by simple adjustments, he can use the processes he has already created, we should expect that he would do so. And, like any modern engineer or programmer, we'd also expect him to make the bare minimum number of changes, so that his original creation was preserved as much as possible.

This is, of course, only a conjecture. But if Jesus' parthenogenesis did indeed produce an XX-male, this would have some profound theological consequences. Externally, it is likely that he would show no discernible difference from an XY-male. However, as an XX-male he could arguably be said to symbolically represent females as well as males. And, in a representative way, he would have a link with those who are "different" from the majority, like those with a multitude of different traits that result in their being marginalized, or feeling isolated by knowing they aren't like others.

In ancient Israel, if this condition had been known, he would have been excluded from the Temple as someone of indeterminate gender.[10] This could almost be regarded as a symbolic disability. Theologically, it means that the incarnation involved sharing one of those many minority traits that a large number of people are born with. When they wonder, "Why me?" the knowledge that Jesus also had a genetic trait that made him different from the majority may help to answer that question. It certainly helps to ground the incarnation more firmly into the mess and reality of human experience.

So science and theology may end up helping each other. The biological sciences have now progressed to a stage where we can induce human parthenogenesis; we know the kinds of processes that would be needed to make this viable and how to produce a male. However, it is so unlikely to occur by natural processes that we would have to call it a miracle if it did—and especially if it were predicted before it happened.

If Jesus' virgin birth did indeed happen in the way described here, it would help us understand the magnitude of God's love for us by showing us his involvement in humanity in such a real way. And it may be particularly helpful for those who feel

---

10. The rabbinic interpretation of Deut 23:1. See Tosefta Yebamot 10.2 and Mishnah Yebamot 8.2 (TinyURL.com/tYebamot10-2 and TinyURL.com/mYebamot8-2).

marginalized because they are different, and those who feel they have the wrong gender or simply aren't sure what their gender is.

When I first realized that this was a possible conclusion about the virgin birth, it felt wrong to me, as it may feel to you now. Thinking about it, I realized that it felt wrong because I expected Jesus to be utterly normal. This shows that I share humanity's prejudice against anyone who is slightly different. Accepting incarnation through virgin birth is yet another way that Jesus humbled himself to become fully part of the human condition.

SUMMARY

- Theologically speaking, Jesus had to be fully human in order to represent and save the whole human condition.

- Scientifically speaking, parthenogenesis (virgin birth) is very unlikely but not impossible.

- A parthenogenic baby will always have two X chromosomes, but XX males can be born who are indistinguishable from XY males.

- *Proposal:* Jesus could have been born by a fully human parthenogenic process as an XX male. This would make him even more representative of humanity, including (to some extent) females and those born different in various ways.

32

▾

Conclusions: Surprise, Disappointment, and Hope

I have been excited, surprised, and depressed by the findings in this book. But ultimately, I'm hopeful. We have found that biblical studies and the sciences really can help each other. After all, they both explore a revelation from God.

What has excited me most about this book is the number of sciences that have provided useful information to help us to understand the text of the Bible. The topics that are covered touch on quantum physics, string theory, astrophysics, multiverse theory, astronomy, paleontology, genetics, archaeology, meteorology, animal psychology, neurology, gerontology, paleoanthropology, embryology, computing, statistics, seismology, and even the nutritional analysis of ancient feces (whatever that specialty is called).

The nonspecialist always needs to have a humble attitude toward findings that may have taken experts a decade or more to study and verify. It is easy to dismiss something we don't understand, especially when it doesn't support the view we are trying to defend. Even those working within a specialty may not understand what others in their own field are doing. For example, within my specialty, there are so many subdisciplines that I don't always understand the work being done by my colleagues in the same building. One scholar is currently working on tense values of verbal strings, and another is investigating Akkadian naming traditions—projects that I only vaguely understand. And my colleagues may not understand my current project in computational linguistics—but we are all working within the discipline of biblical studies.

The human race has worked out how to fly to the moon, map its own genome, and teach computers to translate human languages. These achievements were only possible because of interdisciplinary cooperation between hundreds of specialties contributing technology, code, fabrication, and other skills. Bible scholars need to learn from this, come in from isolation, and join with other specialties so that everyone can gain. That kind of cooperation is what I've envisioned in this book.

"EXPLAINING" MIRACLES

One perturbing finding in this book is that miracles can often be "explained"—but I've realized that this is very different from explaining away the miracles. Just because we know how God may have done something doesn't mean that it was not done by God, especially when the event is vanishingly unlikely and yet it occurs at the exact point in time when it is needed.

We've found that the Bible itself sometimes tells us about the mechanism of a miracle—such as the details given about parting the waters for Israel, both when crossing the Jordan and at the exodus across the Red Sea. Exodus 14:21 says God used "a strong east wind all night"—which an ancient reader would regard as a sufficient explanation, though today we have had to do many experiments to figure out what this means. In the case of the Jordan, the mechanism explained at Joshua 3:16 is likely to be understood better by an ancient reader than a modern one. In both cases, the Bible text is willing to explain how God did the miracle and to emphasize the miraculous timing: they happened exactly when "Moses stretched out his hand over the sea" (Exod 14:21) and when "the feet of the priests bearing the ark were dipped in the brink of the water" (Josh 3:15).

The Bible is impressively consistent in its account of miracles. A compilation of books by dozens of authors spanning thousands of years might be expected to include a variety of different assumptions about miracles, and yet their descriptions are consistent. The miracles never involve things popping into existence, or instantaneous movement by dematerializing something in one place and rematerializing it elsewhere. The closest we get to this kind of thing is the multiplying of food by Elijah and Jesus. However, these are not materializations but growth, because they only produced more of what was already at hand. Jesus fed the crowds with bread and fish because these were the only materials available, while Elijah multiplied flour and oil that the widow already owned. Even miracles of healing can be regarded as sped-up normal healing—as we see when Jesus inquired about a miracle's progress and found that the blind man could not yet see properly (Mark 8:22-25). It is as if God speeds up the normal processes such as growth and recovery of health.

An almighty God can do anything, but the Bible describes what he does do. And it seems that God likes to use his creation to carry out his will. When normal processes won't achieve his purpose, he uses a statistically unlikely or a sped-up version of normal. But we never see him pitting himself against the natural processes, like a fictional wizard or alien—even though this might look more dramatic. Of course, we might assume that God does miracles in a particular dramatic way. Augustine did this when he assumed that God works instantaneously, which meant he had to reinterpret the six days of creation as six different descriptions of a single instantaneous act. We can always find evidence to back up our assumptions, but it is more interesting and instructive to follow where the Bible text leads.

SURPRISE

What has surprised me the most is that the literal text of the Bible so often mirrors an agreement with various sciences. Its correlation with nature as we now understand it is often remarkable. The order of events in Genesis 1 follows what we now know of the history of this planet, and the plagues in Egypt are in the logical order predicted by our knowledge of pollution, infection, and infestation.

Any written text has different possible interpretations—as any constitutional lawyer will tell you. Passages such as Genesis 1 have been explored as concrete literal descriptions, poetic imagery, reworkings of ancient mythology, and as theological statements that have no link with the physical world. In this book I have concentrated on the possible literal meanings of the actual words used. This doesn't mean that I reject other possible types of reading, but one has to start somewhere.

The aim of this book isn't to find the "correct" interpretation, but to show that the Bible text can cohere with what we know from various scientific investigations of nature. Of course, if we read Genesis 1 as poetry or mythology, it won't contradict science because it isn't intending to describe the real world. What surprised me was that literal interpretations of the Bible text can cohere with scientific discoveries. When all the ambiguities of a specific text are outlined so that we can see the limited range of possible literal interpretations, one of those literal interpretations almost always agrees with what has been discovered about nature.

It is often difficult to spot the literal meaning because we read the text through the lens of traditional interpretations. In the account of languages confused at Babel, we read that this affected everyone in the *erets* (meaning "land" or "earth"). We assume the literal meaning is "the planet Earth," even though it could also mean "the country"—as it does just a few verses previously. Biblical Hebrew has a vocabulary of eight thousand words compared to the million words of modern English, so ambiguities like this abound. It is all too easy to let tradition decide what the text means, so we have to studiously explore possible alternate interpretations rather than assume our preferred one is correct.

I've been amazed to find that apparently fantastical miracles such as Joshua's long day, the virgin birth, or human resurrection become less strange when we use sciences to investigate the details in the text. Some of the theories in this book will turn out to be wrong—perhaps all of them—but the point is that the literal Bible text does not contradict knowledge gained by modern sciences. Indeed, the details of the text itself sometimes hold the clues that can point to a link with scientific knowledge that no ancient reader could have imagined. And when the passage is reread in this light, it sometimes solves other difficulties that were present in the text.

These types of explanation for miracles do not mean that we can replicate them. However, they do mean that we can confirm they belong to the universe we live in. They stand out from the miracles or wonders that we read about or watch in works of fantasy and fiction. Exploring Bible miracles in the light of modern sciences demonstrates that they can belong to the history of God's work on this planet, because they are clearly part of our reality and not a fictional one.

DISAPPOINTMENT

What has depressed me in these chapters is the entrenched views of opposing camps. For example, when discussing Noah's flood, any suggestion that it may not have been global is regarded by some as failing a test of orthodoxy. On the other side, it is regarded as intellectual weakness to even admit that archaeological evidence may confirm the ancient historical references to a flood that wiped out a civilization. Strictly speaking, the Bible text is ambiguous—though there are severe problems when you try to fit the literal text into the interpretation that the flood was global.

What has caused me the most despair for the next generation of Christians is our attitude toward evolution. Even though young-earth theories rely on a form of sped-up evolution to produce millions of species from the thousands in the ark, there appears to be a ban on the use of the word "evolution" to describe this process—as if the word itself were harmful. The amount of detailed scientific work that is simply denied in the name of Bible truth is shocking to any fair-minded person who starts to examine it. The result is that intelligent and inquiring students end up rejecting the Bible.

I fear that those looking in from outside assume that Christians approach facts and studies in the same way as conspiracy theorists – that is, publicizing anything that fits, and criticizing anything that doesn't.

HOPE

But I am also hopeful. Many Christians now accept concepts such as "we are made of space dust" or "Two percent of our genes come from Neanderthals." They know that this contradicts some interpretations about how God created Adam and Eve, but their experience of Jesus is firm enough to get them past that difficulty. They expect that someone will one day find a solution, just as so many other Bible problems have been solved by studying ancient history, languages, and archaeology.

The chapters that deal with these topics are among the most exploratory and novel—and therefore have a greater chance of being wrong! This is OK, because that's the way that science works, and it should be the way that theology works too. All scientists work hard to undermine what has already been proposed. They do so by finding some facts to show a theory is wrong or that it can be refined in some important ways. Theology, in its most productive periods, has also worked like that. Luther's Ninety-Five Theses were not dogmatic conclusions but proposals and discussion starters. They certainly initiated some productive debates, but they also ignited arguments that were unfortunately resolved on battlefields.

Christianity is now assumed to be against science. This isn't because Christians question scientific theories— scientists also do that, constantly. We are being anti-scientific when we ignore those facts that don't support our theories, because the scientific method has to take into account *all* facts. Many Christians clasp hold of one interpretation of an issue—such as how long creation took or what kind of death started in Eden—and then refuse to consider that this may be wrong, as if their salvation depended on it.

We need to acknowledge the distinction made in the Westminster Confession of Faith between Bible teaching regarding salvation—which it says is "clearly propounded" in the Bible— and other teachings in the Bible, which it says are "not plain in themselves." God has chosen to teach us through Scripture and through creation. When these two are brought together, those things that are "not plain in themselves" can often become clearer. God's revelation is found in both the Bible and nature, so we should not use one to denigrate the other. We can, instead, grasp with eager hands the gift that God has given us, to learn from both the Bible and scientific discoveries—together.

Index

ANCIENT LITERATURE

BIBLE

SUBJECTS & AUTHORS

Printed in the United States
By Bookmasters